# BY G. WILLIAM JONES

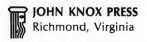 JOHN KNOX PRESS
Richmond, Virginia

# Sunday
# Night at
# the
# Movies

Unless otherwise indicated, Scripture quotations are from
the *Revised Standard Version of the Bible,*
copyrighted 1946 and 1952.

Library of Congress Catalog Card Number: 67–23338
© M. E. Bratcher 1967
Printed in the United States of America
J. 4470

# CONTENTS

# INTRODUCTION

By the time a typical American student graduates from high school today, he has watched more than 15,000 hours of television and has seen more than 500 films. The tv figure is the result of an average of twenty hours weekly viewing for fifteen years, adding up to two full years of 24-hour-a-day televiewing. During the same period of time, this average student has attended school five hours a day, 180 days a year, for twelve years, to produce a total of 10,800 hours of school time. Only sleeping time surpasses television as a top time-consumer.[1]

Church people join with the rest in spending more time looking at films (including TV films) than they do at any other activity aside from sleeping and working.[2]

What do these statements mean to you and to the congregation of which you may be a part? The most characteristic response of the church so far has been silence. The next most characteristic response has been something like, "Well, let's be sure that the church gets her share of the exposure, so we can present *our* side of the story!" A third response, so far the most uncharacteristic, has been a dynamic program of screen education, based on a recognition of the fact that a church called to minister to the whole man will consider as tremendously important the growing percentage of man's life spent in viewing screen productions. Such a church would institute programs to help persons deal more responsibly, creatively, and discriminatingly with the increasing wealth of viewing-life coming to them on the tube and the screen.

The man or woman on the job is finding the screen becoming more and more a part of his pre-service and in-service training. The woman at home watches TV while she irons, sews, or cooks. The child in the classroom sees educational films and watches educational TV for a greater and greater percentage of his study day. The average family spends more of its "together time" in front of the TV set than in any other activity; and when the family gets a night out, it is usually to go to the movies. All of this screen exposure is combining to produce a new type of human culture in the last half of the twentieth century—a "screen culture." Basic to the characteristics of a screen culture are a high degree of sensitivity and an openness to visual communications. A screen culture also finds an increasing percentage of its total life experiences becoming *vicarious* experiences gained through empathetic viewing of screen productions. As was the case before Gutenberg and his associates made printed matter available to the total populace, the masses of people are now returning in great degree to a situation in which much of their information is received in the less abstract and more immediate audiovisual forms best exemplified by the screen media of motion pictures and television. This does not mean that the public is becoming less sensitive to the printed page, but that it is now becoming even more sensitive to the message which is presented in pictorial imagery. The language of our time is increasingly a pictorial language.

The irony of the church's contemporary situation—in the midst of this burgeoning screen culture—lies in our continuing assumption that the truth which we have in Christ can best (or only) be communicated verbally and through the printed page. The church remains largely captive to the prejudice that the Word can best be expressed as a system of *words*.

In preliterate cultures, the church depended greatly upon visual forms for the communication of her message—witness the visual parables of Jesus (the withered fig tree, dining with Zacchaeus, the woman taken in adultery, etc.) and the morality plays of medieval times. Today, when even literate cultures are coming to depend more and more upon visual forms of communication, the church must once again learn to utilize nonverbal and primarily visual forms in the proclamation of her faith.

It is not enough, however, for the church merely to learn how to utilize the screen for her own purposes. In order to respond fully to the challenge inherent in the radical expansion of screen culture in our day, the church must also help to create a public which knows how to respond critically, discriminatingly, and discerningly not only to her own screen productions, but also to those of "the world."

This book is offered in the hope that it may be of some assistance to the church as she goes about fulfilling both of these important tasks.

*Intruder in the Dust* (Films, Incorporated)

# 1. THE SCREEN: A COMMUNICATION BLOCK-BUSTER

One of the most exhilarating events in a person's life may come as he begins to realize that the gospel of Jesus Christ is about himself and his everyday reality. Before this, he may have received the impression that the gospel is only some petulant should-be's on a plane of existence far separated from where people live, and referring basically to a time either far past or far in the future.

But some of the most frustrating and disappointing events in such a person's life may happen as he seeks to share this realization with those who hold his former impression of the gospel's isolation from present experience.

What is the church trying to do when we seek to proclaim the Good News of Jesus Christ in a worship service, a study group, or a simple one-to-one conversation? Are we not simply trying to help persons to come to their own conviction that in the life, death, and resurrection of Jesus of Nazareth we have the whole truth about life presented to us, ready to be examined, understood, decided upon, and lived?

But how does anyone become convinced of this seemingly simple proposition, not just to the degree that he gives mental assent, but to the degree that he realizes how radically it interprets, affects, and challenges his everyday experience and the entire direction of his life? How does a person come to decide that this word is *the* Word about, to, and for his life and his world? What is the church called upon to do in this process?

Several years of experimentation in the use of film and television productions in church groups, followed by interpretive discussions, have convinced me that the screen arts offer at least one way of enabling people to come to a decisive confrontation with the Word of Life.

It would be a gross misrepresentation to claim that the screen arts, even when ideally used, can be some sort of automatically effective "gimmick" which will drive home to people the truth of Christ's claims about themselves and their world. Whether a man decides for or against the Christian proposition is a matter that lies ultimately between him and the spirit of Christ—the One that "enlightens every man." But there are certain man-made obstacles to the faithful, relevant, and vivid proclamation of the gospel that can be greatly reduced—if not obliterated—by an imaginative and dedicated use of mankind's newest art form.

### THE WORD AND WORDS

The church in every age faces a continual need for translating her traditional "in-words" into the most meaningful "in-words" of the society with whom she wishes to communicate. Without translating the timeless Word into timely words, the church can only hope to communicate readily with the few who already understand and appreciate our traditional words and symbols. However, if the church can find appropriate words and symbols of the present which can adequately convey the gospel, then we can communicate with a vastly multiplied group.

As an illustration of this need for translation, take the description of what may take place as a person encounters Christ in his life—or the "Christ-Event." In the traditional verbal symbols of the church, the Christ-Event may be expressed as: "upon seeing his own life in the light of the life of Christ, man knows himself to be a sinner and knows that his life is not life, but death. As a gift of God's grace, he is given the choice of whether he shall remain dead or repent and choose life. If he chooses life, his old unlife of sin is crucified, and he is resurrected into a new life which is the true life, 'eternal' life." Such a rendition of the old, old story might draw a chorus of hearty "Amen's" from Bible students and regular worshipers (although they might not be too sure about what some of the words *mean* in terms of their actual experience), but the majority of hearers might be very discouraged by the special language.

In abridged form and in language most common, however, the

same Christ-Event could be expressed as: "the confrontation of a man by the truth about who he is, how he lives, and what life truly is and is to be lived. Once this is realized, the man chooses either to continue his inauthentic life or else to turn away from his phoniness to embrace and to seek to live by the truth. In turning toward the truth, his old life becomes almost impossible to return to and he begins a new life which is life indeed." Presented in this "secular" fashion, there is a good chance that the "secular man" may be able to hear the story, and to relate to it. If he does, and if he comes to a congregation to learn more about it, then there should be plenty of time to propose to him our belief that Jesus of Nazareth, a historical personage, embodies this "truth about life," and to explain why we call a man's waking up to the truth "death and resurrection."

The church's job of translation is not finished, however, with translating the special language of the Bible and Christian worship into the common language of everyday life. The church must also find ways to show that such words as "grace," "faith," "forgiveness," "*agape*," and "justification" are not just words about what happened 2,000 years ago or after one dies, but refer to here-and-now experiences that take place in each person's everyday life! But how are we to do this? Ideally, we might have a group of people follow a man around day and night, watching his experiences closely, until they could say, "There! There is God's grace operating in his everyday life!" or "There! Did you see what that other person did for him? That's *agape!*"

This approach is rather impractical, but there is another method of bringing a "slice of life" to a group of people with almost the same desired effect—through the screen. Any motion picture or television production which has the integrity to present human life as it truly is, without sloppy sentimentalism or cynicism, and showing characteristic difficulties of relationships without offering "pat" answers, offers us the possibility of seeing the incarnate Word in even the most mundane human experiences. It need not be a church-sponsored or church-produced film to lend itself to this use. In fact, many church-produced films fail most miserably to meet the above criteria for usefulness.

### PROCLAMATION AS DIALOGUE—NOT MONOLOGUE

We in the church often have a habit of speaking before we listen to those to whom we are speaking, and perhaps we never listen at all. This is not only rude and arrogant, but also exceedingly fruitless. We assume that we know the universal human concerns, and we speak to men out of that assumption; but our audiences often respond as did the Filipino to the inattentive missionary: "Sir, you are scratching us where we do not itch!"

Any kind of fruitful communication must be dialogue, not monologue. An attempt to address a man about what is meaningful for his life must begin with *listening* to the man's own statements of his hopes, fears, troubles, joys, frustrations, loves, and hates. There is no element of human life which is foreign to the gospel, no experience that is not finally gathered up in the Christ-Event; but the only way a man hears what this proclamation is saying to him is in relationship to what he *now* feels to be his life situation. Whatever does not deal with or apply to his situation is so much verbiage to him. It is true that the church has only one basic message to proclaim, but there are vast numbers of ways in which to proclaim it, and the ways must be chosen which will *best* communicate to *this* man in *this* situation. To fail to listen to a man (or a nation of men, or a generation of men) and to take his own assessment of his life concerns seriously before we speak to him is to indulge in meaningless and irresponsible gargling.

Within the past several years many congregations desiring to listen attentively to what the world is saying about itself have found that motion pictures and television can enable them to enter more discerningly and relevantly into a dialogue with the world. In every age, man's arts serve as the best spokesmen for his concerns, bewilderments, hopes, and fears. Motion pictures and television, the most characteristic art forms of the twentieth century, may be the best spokesmen for men in our own age, offering us the liveliest opportunities for listening to the self-expressions of those to whom we want to direct our message of faith.

A trend in film-making since the Second World War has moved films toward more realistic treatments of life and the world. Fertile

Hollywood takes a new tack—
from escapism to social confrontation

*On the Waterfront*
(Audio Film Center)

*Advise and Consent* (Swank Films, Incorporated)

insights into large-scale social problems and small-scale interpersonal problems may be gained from sensitive viewing and discussing of such works. For instance, a church group meeting to discuss the topic "Christian Ethics in Business" may have a tendency to oversimplify the ethical problems faced by businessmen and may feel quite satisfied when they arrive quickly at a few easy answers. However, if the group has their discussion following a viewing of a film like *Patterns, The Man in the Gray Flannel Suit,* or *Madison Avenue,* there is a good chance that they will see the problems of business ethics in all of their confusing complexity, and that they will have to wrestle much longer and harder in order to come up with any possible solutions. An address to the business community, then, which grows out of this kind of serious consideration and agonizing will have a far greater ring of authenticity. This is, of course, only one of many possible areas in which the church could use films and television as a means of listening to the world before attempting to prescribe for it out of the riches of the Christian heritage.

### EXPLICITNESS AND IMPLICITNESS

"Why do you speak to them in parables?" Jesus' disciples asked him.

"This is why I speak to them in parables," he replied, "because seeing they do not see, and hearing they do not hear, nor do they understand." [3]

On the surface, these words from the Gospel of Matthew seem to say that Jesus used parables in order to cloud men's minds. But anyone who has tried to proclaim the Christian message to people knows that Jesus was not talking about the desired effects of his parables, but about the status quo of his usual listeners. We face the same communication problem today in that people can sincerely say, "Oh, I see!" when, in fact, they do not see. They may hear the words of the gospel without hearing the gospel itself.

Apparently, the simplest way to convey a truth about life to another person is to state that truth in a short sentence of a few, simple words—a propositional statement. However, Jesus' use of parables is an eloquent witness to the fact that the truth of the gospel does not always lend itself as well to explicit propositional statements as it does to narrative descriptions of common experience in which the truth is implicit. Explicit, propositional statements carry a kind of frozen finality to them, which invites their hearers merely to give either mental assent or rejection. Parables, however, are received by the hearer as a challenge to his own imagination, inviting him to rummage about in them until he comes up with the truth *himself*. Note the vast difference between being told, "Loving your neighbor means going out of your way for *any* person whose need is revealed to you," and being told the parable of the good Samaritan. With the former approach, one can only respond with a relatively passive "I see," or else a petulant "Impossible!" The latter approach, on the other hand, reaches out to involve the hearer in a search for the truth hidden in the narrative and encourages him to form his *own* explicit statement of that truth.

The truth which the church seeks to proclaim is above all, as Dr. Ross Snyder puts it, a "participating-in kind of truth," and therefore requires a manner of presentation in which the receiver is given room and a share of the work (or interpretation) to do. It does not become *his* truth until he has a part in the formulation and expression of it. In view of this, any attempt to "nail down" the truth of the gospel by reducing it to propositional statements, stated as explicitly as possible, may well render the whole communicative effort futile by dooming the Word of Life to being received as a clutter of data. It may be that only the approach which calls forth the most critical and creative powers of the receiver can be the vehicle of the kind of truth which the church is ultimately concerned to communicate.

The closer a screen artist comes to presenting the reality of human experience upon the screen, the better his work can serve the church as a parable—a narrative description of common experience in which the truth is implicit. If we can learn to utilize the screen as a source of contemporary parables, then our process of Christian witness and education can become less a matter of saying, "This is what life means. Take it or leave it," and more a matter of saying, "This is what life looks like. What do you make

—and deeply personal confrontation.

*Cat on a Hot Tin Roof* (Films, Incorporated)

*Tea and Sympathy* (Films, Incorporated)

*The Last Angry Man* (Swank Films, Incorporated)

of it?" The virtue of this second approach is that in the viewer's act of extracting the truth from the screen narrative, and formulating and expressing it for himself in group discussion, the truth will become *his* truth and not just a string of words which he has accepted from someone else.

### KNOWING AND BEING

As Søren Kirkegaard reminded us, to be a Christian is not just to *know* a truth, but to *be* a truth. A person cannot receive the truth fully in a mere word-package, nor can he continue in that truth if it is only a propositional statement in his memory. He needs to have an experience of that truth for himself, which includes confrontation by it and wrestling with it until it yields up its meaning to him. The history of the church shows very clearly a recurring pattern of the way in which men *become* a truth. First, there is the experience of a person or a group of persons which radically challenges their former ways of being. It is only after such an experience, as they try to discover its significance for their lives and seek to communicate it to others, that they begin to construct doctrinal formulations.

The first disciples were able to "turn the world upside down" because of their experience of the life, death, and resurrection of Jesus of Nazareth. In the cases of Luther, Calvin, or Wesley, the doctrines that they proclaimed grew out of their experience of the living truth of those doctrines; the doctrines did not give birth to the experiences. Hence, our attempt to train modern disciples who can turn the world upside down is bound to be frustrated if we expect to do it merely by filling their minds with verbal propositions. If we do this, we are ignoring the lesson of our heritage by attempting to by-pass the necessity of the generative experience which must come prior to the elucidative doctrine. In other words, the "answer" of Christian doctrine makes no real sense until a person has had the experience which raises the "question" for him.

But how is the church to provide such question-raising experiences? Many possibilities are being tried out as the church of today seeks an experience-centered curriculum of Christian education: role-playing, field trips, and a wealth of ingenious group-involvement processes. One of the most effective means of providing a "portable group experience" is the motion picture. The viewers of a well-made dramatic or documentary film do not merely watch the screen characters, they actually identify themselves with the characters and experience their actions and reactions with them. As an example, the viewers of the film *Gentleman's Agreement* have a vicarious experience of how it feels to be treated as a second-class citizen. A vicarious experience does not provide as much motivational force as a direct experience, but it is usually more available. Such a vicarious group experience as a film-viewing can provide a foundation upon which some sound insights can be built as the group thinks through the meaning of their common experience in the light of the gospel. Positions thus arrived at are far more likely to become a part of people's total *being* than of their *knowing* only.

### THE IN'S AND THE OUT'S

The problem of communicating the Christian faith cannot be considered fully until there is some realistic thinking about *to whom* the proclamation is directed. The first and most obvious fact is that the gospel is being proclaimed to each of us all of the time by the very experiences of our lives. Since the Word of Truth is "a two-edged sword," no one ever proclaims it to another without in the same act calling down its judgment and promise upon himself. But, beyond these readily obvious points, it must be said that those who claim priority as targets of the church's proclamation are those millions who have never bent a serious ear to the gospel, whether they be within the church or outside of it.

The problem of communicating with these myriads is complicated by the fact that there are at least three different species of them. To use the terms of the late Paul Tillich, there are the "genuine rejectors," the "non-genuine rejectors," and the "non-genuine acceptors." The first two groups are usually found outside the church; but the third group is most likely found inside the church. They all bear in common the assumption that they have heard fully the Word of Christ and have decided upon the basis of that assumption whether or not they will give it mental assent.

The genuine rejectors are those who *have* heard the Word fully and considered diligently its implications for their lives but have formally rejected it. The non-genuine rejectors are those whose assumption that they have heard all there is to hear about Christ and his gospel is incorrect. All that they have heard has been a very lifeless, vague, and distorted version of the gospel, and they have accepted one or more of the pop-religious concepts of Jesus as the whole truth about him. Ironically, what the non-genuine rejector cites as his reasons for rejecting the church and its message is more than likely what the essential church rejects, too (such as prudish moralism, irresponsible rejection of worldly responsibilities, legalism, spiritual conmanship, etc.)—but he does not know it. If he were to hear the whole, undistorted truth of the gospel, he might be immediately and deeply impressed by its meaning for his life. But how does the church gain another audience—a fresh hearing—from those who assume they have already heard all there is to hear?

The non-genuine acceptors are those within the church who carry the words of the Christian proclamation around in their heads like a baby carries a marble in its mouth, feeling satisfied that they "have it," yet never absorbing it. When the Word is proclaimed to them, they seem to be able to gulp it down easily, but with no change of values, attitudes, or actions. These non-genuine acceptors are able to exhibit such paradoxical behavior because they have never bothered to figure out and act upon what this message actually means in all its ramifications for the daily lives of themselves, their neighbors, their cities, their nations, and their world. Again the question arises: How does the church get a fresh audience—a hearing as for the first time—from those who seem to be impervious to the usual preaching and teaching?

From the late 1700's through the early 1900's in this country even the rejectors of the gospel came to the church buildings or brush arbors to hear an occasional proclamation of the church's message. But today, there are many other forms of diversion, even in the smallest village, to divest the rejectors of their spare time and we are not likely to see them in a conventional worship service or church school class.

The screen, however, is a channel of communication which is open equally to both those inside and outside the church. Television and motion pictures constitute a veritable "hot line" into almost every person's attention in our land. If the church is to find a new hearing from both the rejectors and the non-genuine acceptors of her gospel, it may well be in or through this existing and open channel of communication.

To the non-genuine acceptor, seeing the church's traditional faith couched in terms of a contemporary movie or a television play will certainly be a challenge to a verbalistic faith which has been kept walled off from life's experiences. If accepted, the challenge may lead to a chain reaction of vital associations between his long-known Word and its new-found relevance for his existence.

To the non-genuine rejector, seeing a film like *Cat on a Hot Tin Roof*, and then hearing a discussion about how the basement scene is a near-perfect exposition of the kind of love which the gospel calls for, may be a real eye-opener, causing him to have to reassess his attitude toward the gospel and the church. "So *that's* what you guys have been talking about!" has been a very characteristic response when this approach to the outsider has been taken.

It is only when the church has done its utmost to afford persons with the fullest possible exposition of the gospel as a basis for their free, responsible, and genuine decision that the primary task of the church can be said to have been fulfilled for those persons ("primary" because the church continues to have a responsibility even to the genuine rejectors of the gospel). This is, obviously, a task which will continue throughout the whole life of the person, as succeeding layers and areas of his experience are exposed to the inferences of the Christ-Event; and—just as obviously—a task in which the church must search for the best use of all existing and emerging means of communication. The screen arts will certainly never replace any more traditional form of the church's communication; but they promise a vastly expanded ministry if the church is willing to discover how to use them wisely and sensitively.

*Orphans of the Storm* (Audio Film Center)

# 2. THE CHURCH AND THE SCREEN: A SHORT HISTORY

The church and the screen have been friends longer than they have been enemies.

As early as 1898, the church was giving its enthusiastic support to one of the first "foreign films," a cinematic version of a Passion play staged the year before in Höritz, Bohemia. In 1912, *Ben Hur* and *Quo Vadis?*, both feature-length dramatic films from Italy, captivated the interest and applause of church groups all over the United States. Exploiting the interest engendered by these two epics, American entrepreneurs followed quickly with *Story of Esther* and *Jesus of Nazareth*. The year 1913 saw the beginning of church-sponsored films when a Presbyterian Board of Publications commissioned the Edison Company to do a series of religious motion pictures. The same contract called for the Edison Company to install motion-picture projectors in many of the denomination's churches.

The years from 1898 to 1913 were the beginning of the motion pictures which we still call "religious"; one type made by commercial studios which parlayed the vague religious sensibilities of the masses into box-office fortunes, and the other type made by the churches largely for the instruction and edification of their own members.

By 1920, the *Literary Digest* reported that no less than two thousand churches were using films as a part of their programs of Christian education. The motion picture had been firmly established as a vital part of the life of church members, both within and outside the walls of their meeting-places.

On the other hand, the church's enmity and distrust for the nonreligious or "secular" film (the other main branch of filmdom

The films of D. W. Griffith marked the beginning of today's screen technique. Griffith's innovations became the foundation-standards of the work of later film artists.

*Broken Blossoms*
(Audio Film Center)

*Intolerance* (Audio Film Center)

as seen from the churchman's point of view) probably dates back to 1903, the year of the first widely accepted American story film, *The Great Train Robbery*. *The Great Train Robbery* was not likely to have raised any great disapproval from the churches, but consider some of the titles which followed in the wake of that film's success: *Beware, My Husband Comes*; *The Bigamist*; *Curse of True Love*; *College Boy's First Love*; and *Gaieties of Divorce*. If the film-makers had discovered earlier with the Passion play that American audiences were highly responsive to religious subjects, they now found them even more responsive to "naughty" film stories. The concept of the film as an entertainment device (rather than as an artistic medium) had become firmly implanted in the minds of the American film-makers, and almost the sole criterion of a film's quality for them was how large a crowd it was able to draw. As crowds were flocking to the risqué films, more and more of them began to be produced—and the church became more and more suspicious of any but the most overtly Bible-derived films. Churchmen naturally made pulpit protests over such films, saving their praise and recommendations for the "religious" films, regardless of their quality. More vocal protestors were to come from church leaders such as a certain "Dr. Craft" who, in 1920, issued a statement from his offices in Washington where he was lobbying "to rescue the motion pictures from the hands of the Devil and 500 un-Christian Jews." [4]

Movies of the early '30's such as *Virgin Paradise, Scrambled Wives, The Fourteenth Lover, Her Purchase Price,* and *Plaything of Broadway* added fuel to the fires of protest and strengthened cries for censorship. Entire denominations became so incensed at the contemporary film fare that they declared all motion pictures "a work of the devil," forbidding their members to see them.

In 1933, the Roman Catholic cardinal of Philadelphia forbade all Catholics of that city to attend any of the motion picture palaces, and the following year saw the formation of American Catholicism's Legion of Decency, a film-classifying organization which received large support from Protestant and Jewish groups.

Thus, by the early '30's the church in the United States had formed an ambivalent attitude toward the motion picture which

persists largely to the present—an attitude which accepts uncriti-
cally the "religious" productions of secular and church organizations, but ignores "secular" films except when it takes up cudgels
to beat those films which have dealt too plainly with sex or
exposed too much female anatomy. This 30-year-old attitude is
proving itself to be increasingly more self-contradictory, irrelevant,
and untenable today because of the rise in the last two decades of
a brand of secular film which, in its thoroughgoing realism, bids
fair to outdo the majority of religious films in presenting the
gospel—the truth about life. These films also offer the church an
almost unprecedentedly effective means of listening to the self-
expression of contemporary man.

Two factors contributed to a radical change in motion pictures
during the late '40's. The first factor was World War II. After
Belsen and Buchenwald, Nagasaki and Hiroshima, it seemed that
neither the viewers nor the makers of films could quite bear to
return to the frivolousness, irrelevance, and sheer kiddish inanity
of the prewar movies. The public was like a youth who, having
been shocked and sobered by the coarser and more disillusioning
aspects of life away from home, is no longer able to find solace or
joy in his old toys and his old games. What was needed and
wanted by the public was not a newer and more dazzling toy, but
something that could throw light upon the terrible enigma of man
in his relationships with others, with his world, and with himself.
This new disillusionment with the easy clichés and smooth lies
about life, coupled with a fierce and demanding search for deeper
and more reliable realities, was well-met by the "neo-realist" films
which were being produced in Italy even as that country was
digging its way out of its ruins. Directors Roberto Rossellini
(*Open City, Paisan*), Vittorio de Sica (*Shoeshine, The Bicycle
Thief*), and Carlo Visconti (*The Earth Will Tremble*) pointed
their cameras, not at the impeccably-dressed stars wending their
cosmopolitan ways through a cocktail comedy amid lavish sets, but
at bombed-out streets with ragged men, women, and children
(most of them nonprofessional actors) re-enacting the small trage-
dies and comedies of their own so-recent past. Having been held
back so long upon wide shots of broad, madcap superficialities, the
cameras now zoomed in for extreme close-ups of the daily proc-

esses of the most common life possible, as if seeking at the roots of human experience answers to the question on everyone's mind: "Who are we really? What is it all about?"

If the neo-realist films erred in the representation of reality, it was in the direction of the over-drab and the over-grim. Their thoroughgoing search for unadulterated realism led the neo-realists to reject neat little screenplays in which every action of the characters is self-explanatory, all words and actions drive toward a long-expected climax at the end of the film, and everything finally turns out "all right." Instead, the neo-realists turned out films which were so realistic that they appeared to be "abstract," "obtuse," and "shocking" to many American viewers, accustomed as they were to stylized and romanticized screenfare. For a person who had come to the theatre to be entertained, it was shocking to be confronted instead. Their faithfulness to actual human experiences did make such films subject to varying interpretations, but only in the way that the everyday experiences of our lives are subject to varying interpretations. If such films were difficult to understand, it was because life itself is more difficult to understand than an over-simplified story *about* life.

Europe was again the scene of great innovations in the film during the later '50's, this time from a crop of young French insurgents, the "new wave." Such directors as Jean-Luc Godard (*Breathless*), Francois Truffant (*The 400 Blows, Jules and Jim*), Alain Resnais (*Hiroshima, Mon Amour; Last Year at Marienbad*) and Agnes Varda (*Cleo from 5 to 7*) rebelled even further against traditional domination of the film by predictable and unambiguous stories. They preferred instead to burrow inexorably into the most private recesses of the human mind and behavior, revealing in a cold light the ambiguity, self-centeredness, and inner bankruptcy which they saw in so many of their contemporaries, as well as in the whole scope of world affairs. Their films were likely not to be stories at all, but slow-moving stretches of human interactions combining a sense of listlessness with a countersense of impending doom.

Such films as those of the neo-realists and the new-wave directors were not pretty, nor were they entertaining in the accustomed sense. They were, however, bitingly true to the human experience,

The Italian "neo-realists" utilized non-actors and the real scenes of post-World War II to produce films whose hard-bitten realism was a complete departure from earlier films' glamour and "slickness."

*The Bicycle Thief*
(A Brandon Films 16mm Release)

*La Terra Trema* (Audio Film Center)

The "new wave" of young French
directors in the '50's rejected the
neat screenplays for filmic
experiences that came closer to
the enigmas of human experience.

*The 400 Blows*
(Audio Film Center)

a revelation of what we usually like to ignore or deny about ourselves. Motion pictures were making good on their claim to be man's newest art rather than merely an entertaining toy.

The other factor leading to the change in motion pictures since the '40's—especially in the United States—was the rise of television. Before television achieved its first nationwide audience in the early '50's, American film producers were able to operate upon the sure expectation that a comfortable profit could be made from almost any 90-minutes' worth of film they were able to put together, providing it starred one of the current box-office favorites. The movies had a captive market in the entertainment-hungry and largely uncritical audience, who went habitually to the movies once or twice a week. The advent of widespread television, however, demolished the Hollywood film-makers' utopia. Once people were able to get "for free" on their television screens the kind of entertainment they had formerly paid the motion picture theatres to give them, they no longer needed to venture from their homes at night. In a rising panic over the "TV menace," Hollywood saw that it was going to have to begin producing something new, something different from what the populace could see on television. They tried several gimmicks, including "3-D" and wrap-around screens; but even these were not enough to bring the people out of their dens for long. A few perceptive film-makers began to see that no new gimmick used in presenting the same old kinds of film stories was going to recapture their audiences, but that a new brand of story, acting, and directing was needed. Agonizingly aware of the inroads in their dwindling markets which were being made by the more serious and realistic "foreign films," some Hollywood film-makers decided to try their own hands at film realism.

What issued from these momentous decisions was a heretofore almost unseen product from Hollywood. A trend toward rather unequivocal presentations of contemporary social problems had begun in the late '40's with *Boomerang* and *Gentleman's Agreement* (on anti-Semitism), *Home of the Brave* and *Intruder in the Dust* (on white-Negro prejudice). This trend became not only Hollywood's answer to the TV menace, but also the United States' contribution to the maturation of the film as an art form, as it continued the trend with such socially important films as *Compulsion*, *On the Waterfront*, *The Man with the Golden Arm*, *The Defiant Ones*, *On the Beach*, *Executive Suite*, *I'll Cry Tomorrow*, and *Something of Value*. Interpersonal relationships, especially those between husband and wife, were to receive searching treatment in *Cat on a Hot Tin Roof*, *Dark at the Top of the Stairs*, *All About Eve*, *Hot Spell*, *Tea and Sympathy*, *The Visit*, *Blue Denim*, and *Sons and Lovers*.

Not only was the basic subject matter of these films more vitally important in human affairs than any but the most unusual American films had been before, but also the treatment was less likely to be sentimentalized, as had been the case frequently when Hollywood had previously ventured to treat a "controversial" subject. Following the cue of the Italian neo-realists, Hollywood cameras also turned from a strict diet of superficiality and sentimentalism to more and more ventures into the depths of the human personality and to some unswervingly honest portrayals of the ambivalence of human relationships. In short, some Hollywood film-makers saw that the best direction for the future lay in seeking to portray something closer to the truth of man's experience in the world, rather than merely to provide idealistic or sensationalistic escapism.

In turning from sentimentalism to realism, from the outward and impersonal to the inward and personal, the film industry garnered a new audience which it had not bid for and from which it probably expected nothing but protest—the church. The new direction of feature film-making provided an artistic expression of genuine value to the church, not only as a means of listening to what the world was saying about itself, but also as a means of expressing the meaning of the church's message in life-centered parables.

This is still somewhat of a surprise to Hollywood. When movie moguls think of the "church market"—as some of them sometimes do—and of what will appeal to it, they still seem to think only of biblical stories treated in literal fashion (*The Ten Commandments*, *King of Kings*) or of more contemporary presentations in

*Cleo from 5 to 7* (Audio Film Center)

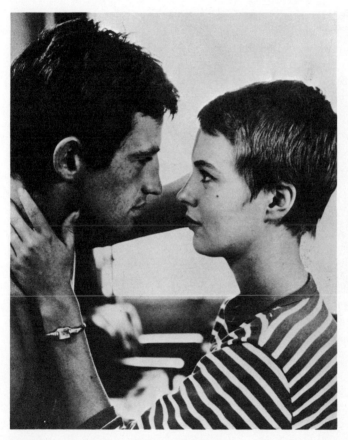

*Breathless* (A Brandon Films 16mm Release)

which missionaries or ministers wrest a fleeting triumph for spiritualism over modern materialism (*Going My Way?, A Man Called Peter*). At least this was their unchallenged opinion until 1965, when one of the awards of the Broadcast-Film Commission of the National Council of Churches went to *The Pawnbroker*. If the message was not strong enough, it was given further emphasis that year as the National Catholic Office for Motion Pictures (successor to the Legion of Decency) gave its 1965 acclaim to *Darling*. Both of these films had been thought of by the general public not only as exemplary works of the cinema's art but also as two of the more daringly realistic films of the year. The B.F.C.'s affirmation of *The Pawnbroker* was especially significant as a signal of the church's new attitude toward the movies in view of the fact that the same group did *not* give an award to 1965's *The Greatest Story Ever Told*.

A new day in the church's film appreciation is being shown by the many pastors now advising their flocks from pulpit and by church newsletter to see the latest worthy films at the local theatres. The doors of parish churches, long closed to any but the most orthodox of church-sponsored films, have swung open in many places and among many U.S. denominations to sixteen millimeter prints of contemporary secular feature films, which are shown and then discussed by the congregations as an exercise in relating faith to life.

Not only is there ample witness to the beginning of a new attitude of the church toward some realistic commercially-produced films, but if *Parable* (a film commissioned for showing in the 1964 World's Fair Protestant Pavilion) is any indication, the church may now be willing to produce or sponsor the production of films in which the approach is not cloyingly sweet, nauseatingly unrealistic, or clumsily explicit. There is also a heartening trend among denominational film producers to avoid the pitfalls of phoniness inherent in the low-budget dramatic films by diverting their main attention to the production of the religious documentary film, which utilizes the actual persons in their actual setting in order to present the realities of the world's challenge to the church's ministries.

If the church is beginning to wake up and take more serious notice of the motion picture (and television), then perhaps it is time to think seriously about possible standards for responsible and creative criticism, on the part of Christians, of both our own and others' screen productions.

# 3. AN EXPERIMENT IN CHRISTIAN SCREEN CRITICISM

> Many people, in their appreciation of life and the pleasures
> that life can give, including the pleasures of man's own creative
> imagination, exist in a mental and emotional fog. The object of
> criticism is to dissolve that fog so that things stand out, sharply
> and clearly defined. Of course, one result will be that much that
> was before tolerated, and thought to be enjoyable, can no longer
> be accepted; the rest, however, will yield pleasure of a richness and
> intensity never previously suspected.[5]

Contrary to the above statement, there are many people who
feel that becoming a "lay screen critic" would not enhance their
enjoyment of screen productions, but would destroy it. Even these
people, however, would have to agree that every person who views
films or television is *some kind* of a critic, if only when he says, "I
liked it," or "I didn't like it." If the role of screen critic is
inescapable for most of us, then the question that still remains is
whether or not it is worthwhile to try to be a *good* screen critic.

There are several reasons why responsible persons of the twentieth century can no longer afford to continue having a superficial
attitude toward the screen. One reason is that television and the
motion pictures are slowly and fragmentarily—but constantly—
moving from being mere "screen media" of entertainment and
advertising toward being the "screen arts." If they are to succeed
in their push toward maturity, these newest arts of mankind need a
public which receives and criticizes them as art. The screen needs
viewers who expect artistic quality from the screen and then
applaud or protest on an artistic basis.

A second reason why viewers need to understand something of
the process of screen production is so they may become aware of
the exact content and purpose of the screen communications
which are directed toward them. A film purporting to be an

objective report of some civil disturbance may actually be a very subtle piece of slanted propaganda, or a television commercial which seems to be selling hair oil on the basis of the product's own virtues may actually be a subliminal appeal to the male ego and sexual drives. Even if it were desirable to eliminate propaganda and subliminal appeals from the screen, it would be impossible. Therefore, the viewer needs to be able to discern these elements as he sees them. Becoming more sensitive to the various motivational uses of the screen is relatively easy, but it takes some study and practice.

A third reason applying to those seeking to be responsible Christians in their attitude toward the screen is that the "people of God" have a mandate to become discriminating and aware in their approach to the screen arts. Our claim to be the "children of God" demands it. The essential meaning of the Fatherhood of God in the Bible is that men are expected to have the same attitudes of love and concern for one another and for their world as their Father, God, has. Therefore, if God is the great Creator, so should all of his children strive unceasingly to be creative. If it seems to us that God is a painstaking Craftsman in all his works, then it behooves us as his children to be forever dissatisfied with anything but the best quality that we can produce or encourage our neighbor to produce. If men have been set by God upon the earth to "subdue" and "have dominion over" it, this is also a mandate to learn how to command the best use of all the forms of art.

### SCREEN CONTENT

Christians of our generation are becoming increasingly aware that the contemporary arts are pleading the same question the church is committed to holding before society: the question of the essential meaning of human experience. The church is also becoming aware that many of the contemporary artists who are seeking to make affirmative answers to this question are thus out-preaching the church—with its own gospel—even though the proclaimers may not be aware that this is what they are doing.

The faith of the Christian community rests upon the radical

assumption that the life, death, and resurrection of Christ is the norm of authenticity for all men in all times. We have the audacity to claim that, in Christ, we see the truth about human experience—ours and everyone else's. In fact, we go so far as to claim that the very fabric of reality itself is revealed by this Christ-Event. Thus, Christ is not simply a historical figure of two thousand years ago, but also a very present Revealer, Judge, and Redeemer of life here and now. To become more and more Christian, then, means to come more and more to view all areas of existence through the calibrated lens of this central Event of human history. We should not be the least bit shy or apologetic in proclaiming to our society that Christ is the "truth about life."

Some critics have called such views "imperialistic" in that they reach out into all areas of life, including the heretofore secular areas, seeking and finding the Christ-Event even there. It is imperialistic, of course—intensely so. Such imperialism follows inescapably our basic assumption that *all* existence is measured and judged by the norm of the Christ-Event, and not just the "holy areas" (such as "religion," Sundays, worship services, Bible study, marriage ceremonies, funerals, etc.). Giving logical extension to our view of life, we are brought out of the ghetto into the whole wide world, there to see the Christ-Event affirmed and denied—acted out or acted against—by myriads who have never even "heard" of it. If we say that the Christ-Event is the truth about life, and the best description of essential reality available to man, then we are also constrained to say that whenever any artist, politician, teacher, etc., discerns something of the truth about life, then turns to share it with others, he is by implication proclaiming the Christ-Event.

Thus the Christ-Event is for the church not only the norm for judging the difference between the authentic and the inauthentic in human affairs, but also the norm for applying the same judgments to works of art which seek to re-create and define human experience.

To be as specific as possible, let us attempt an experiment in screen criticism. We will use as criteria those things about human nature and the purpose of life and its relationships that are revealed in the event of Jesus of Nazareth.

The criteria will be applied to a contemporary "secular" motion picture. Taking only the story or content for the time being, we will speak of the movie as being "authentic" insofar as it exhibits man's experience as we know it in the Christ-Event, and "inauthentic" or "phoney" insofar as it does not.

First, a restatement in contemporary terms of how we as Christians see the life of man—in eight acts:

1. Man is by nature ambivalent, neither all good nor all evil, but capable of vast variations in both directions through exercise of his ability to make decisions.

2. Man makes his choices on the basis of what appears to him to be good—either for himself only, or for himself and his own group, or for all men. Conflict between men arises when one man's good is another man's evil. Conflict within the individual arises when his goods clash.

3. Man has a genius for self-delusion, with which he is able to make his aberrations appear as virtues, both to himself and (to a lesser degree) to others. Such delusions separate a man from others, from his own true being, and also from the whole basis for his being in reality itself.

4. In his condition of estrangement from basic reality, from the truth about life, man seeks in many necessarily futile ways to escape the pain of his isolation. Rather than "using things and loving people, he loves things and uses people." Thus his estrangement from the roots of his own reality leads him to treat other men in an unrealistic manner, depersonalizing them to the level of things, not men.

5. But reality cannot long be suppressed—it keeps bobbing up to confront the phoney. Each time he is confronted anew, man has the opportunity of choosing to accept or to reject reality. If he chooses reality, he must necessarily let go of the elaborate web of self-delusion out of which he has constructed his quasi-life. So, rather than suffer the pain of the destruction of his laboriously-built structure (and if one part goes, all must go), he more often than not elects to continue in his own brand of unreality.

6. If he chooses reality, however, not only does he "die" to his life of elaborate rationalizations, but he also "rises" to a new life of

integrity, which is characterized by his ability to accept himself *as he is* rather than as he wishes he were. He is consequently able to accept others on this same basis. He begins to relate to other persons as persons, valuing them for what they are rather than for what they can do for him.

7. Experiencing the release that comes with the cessation of any necessity to keep up the tremendous labor of fabrication, the new man is able to receive the experiences that come to him with a new sense of exhilaration—almost of exaltation. Because of his reunion with reality (his own reality, the reality of other persons, and the reality of the universe), he senses his essential kinship with the entire created order, and no longer fears what it can do to him as one would fear a completely alien and dark force. The entire universe takes on a benevolent appearance to him that not even the most painful and disappointing experiences can blur for long.

8. In his latter state as the "new" man, however, man is still man, and this is still just as ambivalent as ever. He is just as capable of good or evil as before, and finds it just as necessary as ever to wrestle with his decision-making processes. But now, his view of the good upon which he bases his decisions is far more likely to be qualified by a search for that which is good for *all* men, for that which is good at the deepest levels of human existence, rather than the merely superficial levels. He is also likely to be exceedingly realistic in his appraisal of these factors.

Now, utilizing these eight "acts" as criteria for content criticism of filmic images of man, let us take a look at a relatively recent "secular" movie—*The Hustler*.

"Fast Eddie" Felsen is an extremely likeable person. He strikes up friendships rapidly wherever he goes; he has original and creative ways of looking at life and a genuine sense of vocation about his daily work. But his daily work is that of a "hustler" or pool shark. He makes his living by preying upon unwary pool players. (Score on Point 1.)

What Fast Eddie wants more than anything else in the world is to beat Minnesota Fats, the reigning top pool player, and to become king-pin himself. This seems to him to be the best possible good for himself. But of course, this would be taken for evil by

Minnesota Fats. This conflicting system of goods and evils is further complicated by the fact that, to Eddie, it not only feels good to win—he secretly finds a lot of unconscious satisfaction in being a loser. (Score on Point 2.)

Eddie likes to think of himself as a winner—a man destined to be at the top of the pool profession. But the truth about Eddie is that he is a "loser"—one who enjoys the sweet pain and remorse of failure better than he likes the harsh pressures of success. So, when Eddie finally gets his long-awaited match with Minnesota Fats, Eddie drinks too much and unconsciously arranges for himself to lose. (Score on Point 3.)

The next morning, Eddie decides to leave town; but he meets Sarah, an alcoholic, who drinks in order to escape the pain of her lameness and her consequent sense of isolation from society. In order to forget momentarily the pain and shame of his own failure, Eddie begins an affair with Sarah. Sarah soon comes to love Eddie, but Eddie merely uses her as a means to his own selfish ends. (Score on Point 4.)

Eddie is confronted with the truth about himself by Bert Gordon, a gambler who has a keen judgment of other gamblers' characters. "You're a born loser," Bert tells him. "Winning can be on your back like a monkey. You'll drop that load, too, when you get a good excuse. All you wanna do is feel sorry for yourself." Eddie rejects this confrontation, however, with the protestation that it was the alcohol which caused him to lose, and not his character—or lack of it. It is Sarah who next confronts Eddie with the truth about himself. Eddie, Sarah, and Bert have gone on a gambling trip. One evening, when Sarah tries to help Eddie by pursuading him to break off his business relationship with the malignant Bert, Eddie savagely rejects Sarah instead. Hurt and in despair, she returns to the hotel, where she finds Bert waiting for her with threats and vilifications. Feeling degraded and cast-off already, she seeks momentary escape from her pain through getting drunk and then giving herself to Bert. Afterward, she commits suicide. Sarah's death is a confrontation that Eddie cannot reject. He knows that he did this to her, and what kind of a person he must be to have done it. In the blazing light of Sarah's death, all of Eddie's fond delusions about himself are dissolved. (Score on Point 5.)

Eddie gets a re-match with Minnesota Fats. But this time as they begin to play, it is a different Eddie. He is no longer a loser, but a new man with the kind of self-confidence that comes from knowing the worst about one's self—and accepting it. Eddie beats Minnesota Fats. Now, he has achieved what he always wanted—his greatest good. But, when Bert insists that, from now on, Eddie is to be "his man" (Bert putting up the money for the matches Eddie plays, then taking a 50% cut of the winnings), Eddie refuses. Bert tells him that refusing means that Eddie will never play big-time pool again; but Eddie still refuses, if it means going back to the same kind of cynical hustling which had caused him to be less than a man and had led to Sarah's death. "Your price is too high, Bert," Eddie says. "Because if I take it [come back to work for him], she never lived—she never died." (Score on Point 6.)

Fast Eddie Felsen walks out of Ames' Billiard Parlor, and away from everything that had formerly meant fulfillment to him. We in the audience, however, get the very strong impression that Eddie will not have less of a life from now on—but more of a life. (At least a partial score on Points 7 and 8.)

As indicated to some degree by this film, not many motion pictures (or TV productions) will encompass *all* of the points. But, to the extent that one or more of these points are present, the church will find such films to be "preaching the gospel" in an implicit fashion. These elements are not restricted to the heavier dramatic productions, either, but may be found in comedy (*I Like Money*) or even fantasy films (*Children of the Damned*).

For some persons, such an approach to the criticism of screen content may raise more problems than it solves. One very good demurral might be: "Isn't this pretty restrictive—accepting as authentic only that which agrees with what we *already* believe? Wouldn't we be imposing a lot of pre-set views upon a work of screen art, rather than humbly listening for what its own views are?" To this might be answered that having one's own views of reality firmly in mind does not preclude the possibility of being open to other, perhaps better views of reality. None of us has such a firm and encyclopedic grasp of the Christian message that a sensitively realistic film could not fill in our blank spots, correct our errors, and show its application to existence more clearly.

Another worthy criticism of the above approach to film criticism might be expressed in these words: "It seems that this expression of the Christ-Event in secular terminology sounds very like some statement which a psychologist, sociologist, or humanist might make about man. If so, then what is so uniquely *Christian* about it?"

Whenever the deepest confessions of faith made by Christians begin to "sound like" confessions of faith made by the world's scientists or artists, there are always at least two possible reasons. One is that Christians have sold out to the alien forces of art and science, and traded their heritage for a mess of artsy, semi-scientific jargon. But there is another possibility—that the gospel of Jesus Christ has so worked its way into the warp and woof of Western civilization that no artist, scientist, or humanist can *help* being influenced by it. If this be the case, then our meeting of minds with scientists, artists, *et al.*, need not be seen as a threat, but as the partial fulfillment of a long-awaited promise—that the Lord-ship of Christ should be recognized by all men.

Actually, of course, there *is* something very unique about the Christian proclamation. It lies not in our description of man and the reality of his world, however, but in our conviction that beneath and beyond this reality is God, the eternal Creator, Sus-tainer, and Giver of life. For us, the "eight acts" of man's existence have *ultimate* significance, because their reality is founded upon God, the Giver and Sustainer of reality. What we see at the seething core of this world's reality is God at work through Christ.

### SCREEN FORM

Up to this point in considering the elements in a Christian style of screen criticism, we have been dealing only with content, "story," with character delineation and motivation. It seems to be the assumption of most viewers, except the minority groups of professional screen workers and "film buffs," that the only concern

*The Hustler*—the "Christ-Event" discernible in a "secular" film.

of the viewer should be whether or not it is a good story. This is a very natural assumption, since the best of the film-makers' techniques are those which call least attention to themselves. But the process of mental maturation has to do, to a great degree, with becoming more and more consciously aware of what has formerly been only in the area of the unconscious. Therefore, a person wanting to be maturely aware of why he responds in certain ways to screen offerings must become cognizant not only of what the screen story says, but also of *how* the screen presents the story.

The solely story-centered attitude toward the screen arts is no longer sufficient for responsible people because, as Marshall McLuhan has pointed out, "the medium *is* the message." It is especially true of television and the movies that as much communication of ideas, attitudes, and feelings is done by the subtler technical processes as is done by the more overt and obvious message or story.

The question of content, or of what the work communicates to its beholder, is actually inseparable from the consideration of the question of form, or of how the work is constructed. In a truly artistic creation, *what* a work has to communicate and *how* it communicates it are one and the same thing. As a negative example, consider a poorly executed film production in which the producers are concerned only with presenting their message visually and care little about camera placement and movement, lighting, the technical quality of sound recording, and editing. A thirty-year-old viewer of the finished product will doubtlessly get a much different message from the one which the producers intended to convey. Even if the viewer had never considered seriously the elements of camera movement, lighting, editing, etc., he would have an unconscious sense of the appropriateness of these elements, developed over almost thirty years of viewing life. Although he could not necessarily point out the reasons for it, his response to the film would probably be a lingering sense of frustration, depression, and a high degree of suspicion for the genuineness of both the producer's message and his intentions. Although the producers were concerned only with content, and not at all with the form, it would be helpful for them to realize that the form of their presentation has not only influenced negatively their intended message, but has actually *been* a part of the content conveyed to the viewer. This perhaps serves to illustrate the mistake of those who endeavor, consciously or not, to separate content from form. It may also illustrate why a responsible person needs to become fully aware of all of the elements of a particular art form which affect his response to it.

In setting down elements of screen form for the nonprofessional critic, it will be neither necessary nor particularly helpful to open the Pandora's box of the intricacies of editing, camera angles, aesthetic lines of composition, etc. For those who are interested in delving deeply into these aspects of the cinematic art, there are many authoritative volumes dealing most adequately with every question and technique of film form. (See Appendix I.)

It will be helpful, however, for the viewer to grasp three basic and interrelated principles which will enable him to do a quite adequate job of analyzing the success or failure of the film-makers' use of these elements.

## 1. Visual Continuity

The reason-for-being of the motion pictures is revealed in their name: pictures-in-motion. The motion picture which best fulfills its form is one which is presented in a way unimaginable through any other form; i.e., in a way which strikes its viewers with the absolute necessity of pictures-in-motion for the conveyance of the total impression that particular film makes. If the impression could be conveyed without the picture, it is a gross mistake to spend thousands of dollars for a film, when a radio program or a tape recording would do the job just as well. If the impression could be conveyed without the motion of the pictures, why not just have a film-strip or a slide-set with recorded or live narration?

The history of motion-picture innovation illustrates the point aptly. To begin with, in 1896, motion-picture audiences were fascinated with the simple innovation of lifelike motion on a screen. In an evening at the nickelodeon, audiences "oohed" at scenes of ocean breakers rolling up to the sandy beach, screamed in genuine terror as an express train bore down upon them, and then were quite happy to watch five minutes of nothing but scenes of couples strolling in a park. By the turn of the century, audiences which had once insisted upon nothing more than unrelated scenes of movement (visual discontinuity) grew jaded. The new visual toy was relegated to the position of "chaser" in vaudeville houses—something to clear stragglers out of the theatre before the next show began. The survival of the film in the United States at this point in history was due to the work of E. S. Porter who, in 1903, produced the first American films in which various scenes, cemented together into one long strip of film, told a story. Porter's first film of this type was *Life of an American Fireman*, followed within a few months by the classic *The Great Train Robbery*. Audiences were not only recaptured by this new concept of the motion picture as visual continuity, but responded with such enthusiasm that the motion picture industry became a firm reality within the next few years.

Although the mushrooming studios were to produce many grossly inartistic films in the quarter-century of silent story-films that followed, the unavailability of sound *forced* them to create film stories whose main line of communication was visual. The later-developing practice of adding titles and accompanying music scores for local theatre piano players did not detract from the visual quality of the films, because titles and music were used to *support* the primarily visual action, and could not *dominate* it.

But the innovation of the "talkies," with Warner Brothers' *The Jazz Singer* in 1927, literally turned previous guidelines of motion-picture production upside down. For several years thereafter, audiences were so enthralled by the phenomenon of larger-than-life projected moving images which *talked* that motion pictures tended to become long gab-sessions which were—incidentally—photographed. A blind man could go to the movies and not miss a thing of importance. Sound became a monster which gobbled up the former mainstay of visual continuity as a dominant force. Rather than sound being used as a contributing support to pictures which were primarily visual in their dynamics, the picture became a relatively pathetic concomitant to productions which were primarily verbal. It was not until 1935 that any semblance of correct balance between sight and sound was to emerge from Hollywood in John Ford's *The Informer.* Sad to say, the creative balance between sight and sound found there, which is most appropriate to the motion picture's forté of visual continuity, was not as well followed as Porter's corrective had been earlier. Sound-dominated, chiefly verbalistic films are still very much with us today.

## 2. *Kinship to Ocular and Mental Patterns*

At its best, the camera is an extension of the viewer's eyes and, behind them, of the viewer's mind. Because of this fact there is a further exercise of realism (in addition to the realism of content) that dictates how the camera is most authentically to "see" its scenes. The basic principle for this realism is kinship to the natural ocular and mental patterns of the viewer.

Again the short history of motion pictures serves to illustrate the point. The first motion pictures were shot by a "paralyzed camera." Unconscious inhibitions of the cameramen and their directors, caused largely by thinking of their productions more in terms of the older art of the theatre than in terms of the newer art of the cimema, led them to establish the use of one unmoving point-of-view for the camera. Limiting the viewpoint of the camera to that of a spectator in the down-front section of a theatre, the camera took up its position in a line directly in the center of the set and fifteen or twenty feet from the action. To enter the scene, the actors had to "walk on" from the off-camera "wings" and exit by walking out of the camera's range. And woe be to the actor whose bit of action caused him to step accidentally out of the camera's range! The camera was not the least bit willing to "turn its head" (or "pan") to place him back in view, even though what he was doing was vitally important to the sense of the scene. Also in the style of the theatre, the actor usually had no opportunity to go back and take the scene over. "The show must go on!" If the actor sat down, the camera would not "tilt" to center him in the picture. If the actor's work for the particular scene was to smirk, he would have to smirk *largely* because the camera would not move in closer (or "dolly in") to concentrate upon his face (a "tight

close-up"). Even in the work of the French pioneer, Georges Méliès, whose story-films antedated Porter's by a good five years, there was undue influence of the theatre shown in his practice of beginning each scene with a curtain-like fade-in, and ending each scene with a fade-out.

By the second decade of the new century, however, the directors and cameramen had realized that their new art need not be bound by theatrical conventions, and the camera was becoming less inhibited in its movement. David Wark Griffith (*The Birth of a Nation, Intolerance, Judith of Bethulia*), the father of modern cinematography, illustrated that the camera could be an extremely active *participant* in the filmed action rather than the static, passive viewer represented by the down-front theatre patron.

Under the creative genius of Griffith, the camera found a freedom to move in closer to the actors in order to catch the subtle but significant flicker of an eye or movement of a hand, to turn or tilt in order to watch a character's movement from one place to another, or to look at the scene from an oblique angle in order to show depth and spatial relations. When the film had been exposed and developed, Griffith would work with his editors to join the shots and sequences together in a style very similar to the natural action of the human eye and mind. From a wide view of a set with three or four characters, Griffith would change the picture instantaneously (or "cut") to one member of the group, then cut again to a close-up of a gun concealed in the character's hand. Thus, the camera eye would duplicate the human eye's manner of orienting itself to a new field of vision, from the general sweep of the scene to a fixation upon the most important detail. Griffith also employed a system of pacing in his editing process which, although he came upon it intuitively, might well have been derived from a modern scientific scrutiny of human visual and mental patterns. For instance, when he wanted to indicate a sense of increasing tension or fright in a character, the segments of film between cuts would become progressively shorter and shorter, as a man under increasing stress might look first this way, then that way, trying to look every way at once in hopes of seeing what was threatening him. Conversely, when Griffith wanted to indicate peace and serenity, the cuts would come further and further apart, giving the camera leisure to survey the scene almost indolently. This technique is a close parallel to the usual ocular pattern of the relaxed person lazily "staring into space."

D. W. Griffith is also credited with being the forerunner of modern motion-picture editing because of his manner of composing a scene from short bits of film which were shot from different distances and angles, then put together. Although some of his contemporaries predicted doom for his films because of his unorthodox practices, Griffith's method became established as the basis for film artistry of the future. Why did his method continue, whereas the more theatrical style of using one long, unbroken strip of film, taken from one fixed point of view, died out? Basically it was not only because the films of Griffith presented a visual continuity which was immediately more interesting than the flat, static depictions of earlier directors, but also because the realism of his style so closely followed the customary movements of the eye and the inquisitive probings of the mind. Under Griffith's direction, the camera as representative of the viewer took upon itself the humanized function of a curious, observant participator, who saw each new scene, then moved into it to circle the characters, watching closely their actions and reactions, scrutinizing important objects. Not only was such a camera able to observe the characters externally, but it was also able to penetrate into their thoughts by extreme close-ups of their features or by dissolving the present scene to bring into view the scene they were thinking about. Or sometimes the camera could even *become* the character so that it saw its scenes through the blurred eyes of weeping or the distorted vision of drunkenness or insanity.

The pioneering methods of D. W. Griffith have been refined into systematic and premeditated artistry by later directors, but never surpassed or replaced as a basis for the art of the film.

## 3. *Unobtrusiveness*

It is as true of the art of the film as it is of any other art that a method or artifice which calls attention to itself instead of supporting and enhancing the whole work is anathema. Consequently, in a motion picture the music, lighting, editing, and camera work which are the most invisible are usually the most adept. Their invisibility stems from the fact that they have made their necessary contribution to the film subtly and with just exactly the right emphasis and placement. When they become obtrusive, it is usually because they have been done inadequately or ostentatiously. Of course, a person who embarks upon a serious study of the motion picture will soon become much more aware of these elements than ever before, and may rue the day he began his study, as his heretofore unconscious enjoyment of films is jarred by microphone shadows on the wall, lips moving to different words than those on the sound track, too familiar tunes in "background" music, or "show-off" editing. The serious study of the screen, however, is not meant to destroy the simple pleasure of being caught up in a filmic narrative and swept into an event which broadens one's storehouse of experience. Quite the contrary. It is meant to help one to be able to discern, then discuss, the exact *something* that *prevented* his total appreciation of the film. Or, it may enable him to put a finger on the genius of a film which has afforded him a most rewarding experience. As a person becomes more practiced in his new approach of viewing films critically, however, it is hoped that he will come to the point at which he can let go of his new knowledge, leap into the film experience without reservation, and then be able to direct his critical knowledge upon the film's failures and successes *after* he has seen it.

In view of the foregoing, it appears that there will be different degrees in "invisibility" of production techniques because there will be different levels of awareness of these techniques among the viewers in any audience. There will always be different levels of criticism—from that of the novice to that of the professional critic—but in our society there is hardly ever a viewer who is totally unaware of inadequacy or ostentation in screen productions, because almost every citizen has been absorbing films and television for many years, deriving from his experience an unconscious—if not conscious—standard of adequacy. The main difference between the student of the critical viewpoint and the non-student is that the non-student will be largely unable to discern and discuss what it was that made the film he has just seen an exhilaratingly, inspiringly "good film," or a disappointingly, disturbingly "poor film."

MUSIC: The function of music in the film is, fundamentally, to augment the emotional impact of certain scenes, as well as to provide transitions between scenes. If the music has a repetitious tonal pattern or is likely to be a familiar tune to many of the viewers, it is apt to be distracting and to draw attention to itself rather than to the filmic action. Similarly, if the music is too self-consciously grandiose for a humble scene, so loud that it covers important words or sounds, or creates a mood unrelated to the dominant mood of the scene, it is inadequate—if not damaging to the film. A well-scored film may leave most of its viewers consciously unaware that a good third of the film was accompanied by music, except perhaps for the theme music with which the film began and ended.

LIGHTING: The function of lighting is not only to give necessary illumination to scenes, but also to provide or to enhance moods. Shadows and darkness are in harmony with moods of depression or the sinister, whereas brightness usually supports moods of gaiety and hope. Very few films of today commit the sin of allowing distracting shadows of cameras or microphones to fall upon the set walls or upon actors' faces; but many err in washing out the possible depth of their scenes by using too much and too harsh a light, giving the scenes a flat, two-dimensional appearance. Orson Welles' now-classic film, *Citizen Kane*, used many unaccustomed effects of camera and editing, but was criticized for apparently unjustified use of excessive shadow. Although many other outré effects were used, they were integrated so smoothly and naturally into the fabric of the visual narrative that they did not force themselves into the viewer's consciousness. But the continual use of ponderous shadows even where the mood was not necessarily somber or threatening made many people janglingly aware that they were watching a film and that the director was attempting some very artistic lighting.

CAMERA AND EDITING: The cameraman-director-editor team will occasionally lapse back into mainly pre-Griffith, theatrically-dominated means of presenting the picture, ignoring half a century of progress in the film art. Other such teams may be guilty of excesses in a more futuristic direction by using such devices as repeated "swish-pans" (a sideways-movement of the camera too fast for the eye to follow, producing a smear upon the screen), rapid-fire cuts which flash pictures on and off the screen too fast for the eye-brain mechanism to respond consciously, or completely unwarranted camera angles (camera looking straight down from the ceiling onto the poker table, taking a peep at a motorist through the glass window of a parking meter, etc.). Such devices are self-defeating either because their action is so alien to the human eye's *modus operandus,* or because they are so self-consciously "cute" that they prize the viewer out of the flow of his vicarious experience, calling his attention to the fact that he is now watching—not a representation of life—but a show-piece of directorial genius.

Those seeking to employ the foregoing rules-of-thumb to the criticism of motion pictures and television productions should keep in mind one further consideration. Remember that such rules—like all rules of their ilk—are meant to cover general circumstances, the "usual." Some of the most creative and effective artistry is sometimes accomplished by breaking such rules. The responsible artist, however, must always be aware that there *is* such a rule, that he is breaking it, and must be intentionally breaking it for a greater purpose than he could accomplish by complying with the rule. His public becomes his jury, either captivated or jangled by his venture.

The standards for criticism of film form here presented are predominantly audience centered, growing out of a belief that an artifice is most creatively artistic when it humbly serves the beholder's experience of the work as a whole. Conversely, that artifice which inhibits and disturbs the fullest experience by calling attention to itself or imposing an unnatural hurdle for eyes and minds is the most inartistic.

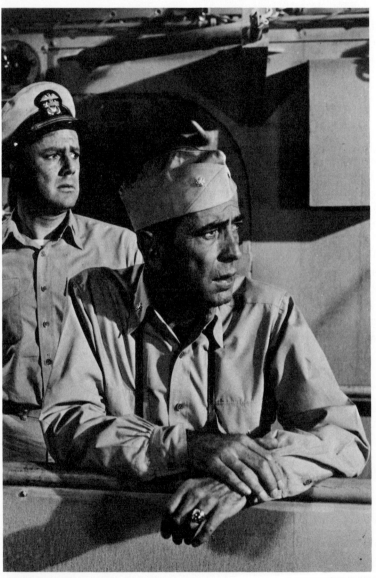

*The Caine Mutiny* (Swank Films, Incorporated)

# 4. DREAM AND REALITY: A PSYCHOLOGY OF VIEWERSHIP

Nothing serves better to illustrate the peculiar potency of the motion picture medium than the uncanny sensation a theatre-goer has upon emerging from an afternoon matinee. He blinks at the sunlight, not only because he has just spent a couple of hours in darkness, but because he is almost resentfully surprised that it is still the same daylight, same street, same hubbub of business activity as it was before he entered the motion picture theatre. He is surprised, somewhat disoriented, and perhaps a little disappointed as he joins the stream of people on the sidewalk, because he has been "away" from all this for awhile, having had a very dramatic experience which has exercised both his intellect and his emotions—and nobody seems either to know or to care about it. If the experience he has just had was an exceptionally strong one, he is filled now with a desire to bear witness to the way in which it has taught him something new about himself or all men, he wants to explore with someone the long-held attitudes of his which have just been challenged, or an old, forgotten emotion which has been stirred again after lying dormant for years within him. But he knows what a fool he would be taken for if he were to catch the next person by the sleeve and say, "Look! I've just had the most amazing experience in there, and I'd like to talk to you about it!" So, with one last look at the stars' pictures on the marquee—the familiar faces of those with whom he has so recently been through all sorts of trials and adventures—he sighs and turns to walk away down the glare-filled, unknowing street.

A few hours later he may not be able to recall the ideas and emotions he was so eager to share with someone as he left the theatre. Ask him tomorrow why his eyes filled with tears at one particular point in the film, and he will probably be embarrassed to admit that the film "got to him," and shrug it off as "just a movie, anyhow."

What, if anything, actually happened to that person during those hours in darkness before the screen? Did nothing happen—a merely meaningless way of killing a few hours? Or was what happened more like a dream, into which he projected some of his fears and desires, and out of which arose some images of life which will continue to haunt him vaguely with promise and threat even after he wakens? Or did he really "have an experience," with a level of involvement and after-effect similar to that of participation in actual events? Perhaps a closer view of factors in the experience of viewing a dramatic feature film will help to illuminate this important question (important if only from the viewpoint that a person driving toward maturity should want to be able to understand the workings and meanings of all of his experiences).

### CHANNELIZATION OF ATTENTION

As a person enters a large film auditorium, lighted for the intermission, his eyes wander in many directions; they sweep the total scene, taking in the architecture, stopping momentarily upon a face or the back of a head that seems familiar, then centering upon a vacant seat at the most advantageous spot. Once seated, the person's eyes will continue to pick and choose among myriad views which the interior of the theatre offers to him. And, as his eyes wander and jump from place to place, so will his attention follow the capricious pathway of his eyes. Where his attention centers, there his mind is almost sure to follow.

There is a direct linkage of operation and function between the mind and the eyes that is broken only during times of daydreaming or inattention. This linkage may operate from the inside out, as when the mind directs the eyes to attention upon some object or scene; or it may operate from the outside in, as some object or scene catches the attention of the eyes. In the latter case, this relationship may be expressed by stating that whatever manages to catch the eye also captivates the attention, and whatever captivates a person's attention usually is given access to his mental consideration. The straightest pathway to the mind is through the eye.

As the lights begin to dim in the theatre, the possible areas of vision are limited more and more until, as the room reaches total darkness, all possibilities of visual distractions (except the man lighting the cigarette three rows down and the couple treading on his toes to get to seats on his row). Distractions reduced to a minimum by the darkness, the screen brightens and the motion picture begins. Now, there is but one field of vision available to the viewer's eyes, the screen. In any given visual field, the human eye is always inexorably drawn to the element within the field which is brightest and/or has the liveliest movement. The screen is the brightest thing in the large auditorium, so it draws the eyes of the viewer; but he still has a pretty large field of vision upon which his eyes might rove and fix at will. Wise movie-makers have taken the habits of the eye into account as they compose their scenes for the camera, light them, shoot them, and later edit the shots into story-telling sequences. They know that the eye, trained almost from infancy to begin reading each page of reading material from the upper left-hand corner, has absorbed from that training the habit of spending more of its attention in each new scene upon the upper half of the field than the bottom half, and more on the left side than the right. Knowing this, and wanting to be sure to capture the eyes of the viewers for the most important elements in their scenes, directors will make sure that important characters, entrances, objects, etc., fall as closely as possible within the upper left quadrant of the screen.

Not only does the film-maker assure himself, as much as predictably possible, of having his viewers' attention exactly where he wants it in a particular scene by having the element in the upper left quarter, and possibly made even more attractive by greater movement and brightness there than among other elements within the scene; he can also direct the viewers' attention even more predictably and specifically by "zooming in" or "cutting" from the larger picture to a close-up of one, minute element of that picture. In a theatrical production, by contrast, the director may assure his viewers' attention to the stage by having a well-lighted stage in a darkened house. He may further direct the viewers' attention to a certain part of the proscenium area by brighter light or greater movement in that area than others; but he can never guarantee himself that his viewer is bound to look at only one face, one hand, a book, or a gun by removing all other elements from the viewer's possible vision. The motion picture director can do this with a simple close-up. This great potential for channelization of attention, with the entré to the mind that goes along with the attention, is one of the foundational strengths of the motion picture.

### SUSPENSION OF DISBELIEF

A second factor contributing to the screen experience is one that stems from our earliest experiences with story-telling. Since the time in our childhood when we first understood that fairy tales and nursery rhymes were not actually true, but wanted nevertheless to experience them fully in spite of our sophistication, we learned to practice temporary suspension of disbelief when we understood that someone was going to tell us a story. Rather than exercising our usual methods of sifting between what we assumed really happened and what did not really happen, we willingly relaxed such judgments for the extent of the story, preferring to let ourselves be delightfully caught up and carried away with the "what if" rather than insisting upon the "what is." We have also extended this dropping of our factualistic guard to include those times we spend before the screen. One of the correctives to this practice, however, is that we suspend disbelief only when we feel that we are being addressed with a screen story which is not a direct record of an actual occurrence (such as a documentary film or newsfilm is). This preserves us from taking too seriously the characters and events of the story itself, while leaving us open to accept or to reject what appears to be the *meaning* of the story. In this manner, we approach a story-film much like we approach one of the parables of Jesus—not becoming involved with the question of whether or not there was a certain unjust judge who actually did relent and change his verdict for an importunate woman, but being open to the truth which the parable carries *within* it. Willing involvement with the "what if" of a true-to-life story may thus throw great light for us upon the "what is."

The problems of honor, integrity, and expediency are examined in films like these, which examine the tensions of man with man, man with his "duty," and man with himself.

*The Bridge on the River Kwai* (Swank Films, Incorporated)

### IDENTIFICATION AND EMPATHY—
### THE VICARIOUS EXPERIENCE

If the drama which the viewer is watching is at all lifelike, the characterizations believable and soundly motivated, and the technical elements adequate but not distracting, a strange thing happens. The viewer does not just *watch* the unfolding screenplay, he *participates in* it!

In the first few moments of a film, the director subtly but kindly (or diabolically, as we shall see shortly) points out to the viewer which character of his own sex is the strongest, most heroic, kindest, most generous, lovable, creative, and funniest. On the basis of his own existing attitudes, the viewer may emotionally "take sides" with the character which best exemplifies his own attitudes. Or, on the basis of his unfulfilled wishes about his own image, the viewer may "identify" with the character who best exemplifies the qualities or accomplishments he himself would like to have. As the action progresses and becomes more involved, so the viewer becomes more involved with his screen-partner until he may actually "empathize" with his chosen screen figure. As this happens, the viewer loses much of his surface self-awareness and, in effect, leaves his seat in the audience to take his place upon the screen in the person of the character with whom he empathizes. From that point on (unless the spell is broken by some jangling, inappropriate element in the film which snaps the viewer back into full awareness that he is merely sitting in a theatre watching a series of projected photographs), the experiences of the screen figure become his own experiences. That is, when his empathetic counterpart is threatened or triumphs, the viewer feels threatened or exults. What the actor experiences directly, the empathizing viewer experiences vicariously through the actor's projected image.

The results of the empathetic experience may be that the viewer has an opportunity to let off some steam by vicarious participation in aggressive behavior; he may be singularly gratified by a shadowy, fleeting fulfillment of his desire for adventure, fame, or adulation; or he may learn something of what it feels like to stand in the shoes of a person of a different time, nationality, ethnic group, or of some other situation vastly dissimilar to his own. In the "stepping outside one's self" which happens in moments of empathetic, vicarious experience, the viewer is given the opportunity to see the world through another's eyes.

This may not always be such a pleasant experience for the viewer. He may, for instance, find himself trapped by a canny script-writer or director into identifying with the supposed hero of the film in early scenes, only to find later that this character is actually the scoundrel or villain of the film story. Similarly, the viewer may be a person with deep racial prejudices, and may find himself with only a Negro hero with whom he can identify (*Edge of the City, A Patch of Blue*). Such experiences, however unpleasant to certain viewers, are not entirely without value.

### MENTAL AND EMOTIONAL RESPONSES
### TO AURAL AND VISUAL STIMULI

Every tyro film-maker knows that he can depend upon predictable audience reactions to various kinds of camera shots, transitions between shots, arrangements of persons or objects within the frame of his picture, as well as to certain kinds of background music, camera angles, and set lighting.

The emotional influence of music and different values of lighting have not only been treated above (see Chapter Three); but they are already a very obvious and familiar factor to most persons. We know how surely we respond to sad or gay or ominous music. We are also familiar with the way in which the sight of a heavily-draped, darkened interior prepares us for scenes of sadness or intrigue, and how a light, airy room leads us to expect comedy and light-heartedness.

A more subtle, but no less effective, bid for the viewers' response is made by the arrangements and movements of elements within the frame of the picture. A picture is an arrangement of shapes, which are made up of elements of line, mass, and form. Our emotional reaction to shapes is very definite and predictable. A set composed mainly of straight lines, for instance, gives the viewers an impression of directness, rigidity, or masculinity. Curved lines, on the other hand, produce an aura of charm, grace, and femininity.

Broken lines in a pictorial composition give an impression of informality, indecision, or disorder. Predominantly vertical lines create a sense of importance, uplift, aspiration, or spirituality, whereas horizontal lines represent repose, tranquility, or stability. Diagonal lines provide an atmosphere of force, action, and aggressiveness.

From the aspect of mass, large, bulky, or looming masses give an impression of strength, power, or threat, while small or isolated masses represent to the viewer a sense of insignificance, loneliness, or fright.

If objects or characters within a scene are arranged in the form of a square, we assume unconsciously that there is an equality of force or interest among them; but if the characters are arrayed in a right angle, we get the unconscious impression of inequality and conflict between them.

The angle between the camera and its subject has a similar effect upon the viewer. A shot taken from a high angle downward upon the subject tends to make the viewer feel that the object or character is weak, lost, or unable to cope with the pressures around it. Conversely, a shot taken from a very low angle up toward the subject gives that subject an aspect of powerfulness and threat, and makes it seem almost invincible.

Any viewer is likely to feel that all is going well when he sees a character enter from the left side of the frame and move toward the right side; but he receives an impression that all is not well when the direction of movement is reversed, from right to left. Armies marching confidently off to battle usually proceed from left to right off the screen; but a defeated army comes back into our view from right to left. The very direction of movement sets up a sense of ominousness and tragedy in the viewer, which is probably another concomitant of our ingrained reading habits.

Orthodox transitions between filmed scenes rely only partially upon the subconscious reactions of the eye-mind apparatus, and are dependent for the rest of their effectiveness upon a subliminal training which film-viewers absorb through many years of motion picture theatre-going. The traditional way of indicating to an audience that a long time elapses between scenes, for instance, is for the first scene to gradually "fade out" into blackness, then for the next scene to "fade in" from that blackness. The audience probably "gets the message" of time-lapse partly because it reminds them of a sleep and partly because they have become accustomed to the use of the "fade-out, fade-in" transition for this purpose. Instantaneous transitions from one scene to another, or "cuts," on the other hand, usually mean to the audience that both bits of action are immediately consequent, if not simultaneous. In the middle of the time-significance of the stock transitions is the "lap dissolve," in which the first scene seems to wash out as the second scene washes in without the screen going black. This signifies to the viewers that *some* time elapses, but not as much as the fade-in, fade-out signifies.

Perhaps it should be reiterated at this point that the purpose of trying to sensitize the nonprofessional screen critic to these usually unnoticed elements of the screen art is not to make him immune to the film-maker's wiles. It is simply to enable the viewer to derive an even richer experience from the best of films by understanding how they produce their good effects upon him, and to assist him in pointing more specifically and knowledgeably to the flaws in the poor films. This is done in hopes that the criticism of a more discriminating audience will spur film-makers to a greater integrity, a greater artistry, than might ever be possible with a largely unsensitized audience.

*Edge of the City* (Films, Incorporated)

# 5. VIEWING AND DISCUSSING A FEATURE FILM

A local church congregation, advised that the Sunday evening program would be a three-hour study on "Problems of Family Life," was surprised to find half of that time devoted to the viewing of a secular motion picture, *Dark at the Top of the Stairs*.

A district youth organization of another denomination, on a weekend retreat to study about "Teen-age Ethics," was somewhat bewildered when the opening event of the retreat was the showing of *Blue Denim*.

A seminary class was unusually gratified with an assignment of extra work when it turned out to be going to a downtown theatre to see *The Hustler*, and then returning to their classroom for a lengthy discussion of what that movie had to say about classic theological concepts, such as sin, grace, death, and resurrection.

Almost all of the people involved in the foregoing events were wondering—at first—why the church would be using up valuable time on a secular motion picture, and what good could possibly come from inviting into the church an entertainment medium that not too many years ago had been considered by many Christians to be one of the prime enemies of the church. They wondered until, following the viewings, they found themselves in a discussion of issues raised by the film, or of their own subjective experiences while they watched. The discussion groups were much like many others in which they had been involved during their lives in the church; but the discussions had a high degree of relevance, seriousness, and the excitement of discovery that had been missing in most of their other group experiences in the church. With good leadership, they found themselves able to talk about life and the gospel of Christ in a manner which was stimulatingly "here-and-now" rather than boringly "there-and-then." After one such experience, an adult church member telephoned his pastor to say, "You've really gotten me hooked with those film discussions! I can't even watch *television* now without seeing grace, *agape*, redemption—and wanting to call up all the other members to get them to tune in and see it with me!" At a retreat in which several films had been used, one teen-ager remarked, "I thought all those words like 'sin,' 'salvation,' and 'resurrection' were just words that adult church members liked to swap around, until I was able to see how they *look* when they *happen* in life." Rather than having to dream up lifelike situations in which the gospel could be seen to apply with specific clarity, participants in these viewing-and-discussion groups had been given a rich fund of common experiences, through their vicarious experience of a film, to talk about and to compare with their own individual experiences. "Referent confusion," the great bugaboo of communication in which different words mean different things to people because of their differing experiences, had been partially and temporarily overcome.

Almost every contemporary church member has had the experience of seeing a motion picture in which he became aware that the basic issues of life were being raised in an incisive manner, or that the Good News itself was being proclaimed on the screen in a secular form. In such experiences, he has had the natural desire to share this Bread of Life which has been broken open for him. He has wanted to talk about the film with others who have experienced it—not in some superficial manner ("Howdja like the picture?" "Fine.")—but in a way that pried all the meat and marrow out of the film, holding it up so that he and his friends could take a good, long, memorable look at the way in which the message of the New Testament enters into life and illuminates it.

The familiar desire to have a rousing and perceptive discussion of a theatrical film in which one has just been deeply involved is usually frustrated. The viewers return home, perhaps swapping a few clichés on the way; but the benefit which the film might have provided as a basis for a systematic discussion is lost. The determination of some churchmen that such a creative potential should not be lost, however, has turned up several ways in which groups may share in both the viewing and the systematic discussion of a beneficial motion picture.

The most ambitious plan for the sharing of a filmic experience consists in arranging with the local exhibitor for a special showing. Most local theatres, particularly those in small towns and with small seating capacities, may welcome the opportunity of providing a special showing of a film which they already have running. (It is somewhat more difficult and more expensive to make arrangements for showing a film which must be special-ordered for only one showing—but not impossible.) They may welcome the opportunity for one or more of three possible reasons: (1) hoping to cement relations between church and theatre, creating a more positive attitude toward the film on the part of a group from which comes many potential censors; (2) having a guaranteed income from a run of their film; or (3) out of sheer curiousity.

Financially speaking, the group which wishes to arrange for a special showing must either be able to guarantee that a majority of the seats in the theatre will be filled (in which case each participant merely pays his own ticket fee), or by the group's paying the exhibitor some mutually-agreeable lump sum which would approximate the sum he might reasonably expect from a normal run. Either of these possibilities may be facilitated by having several congregations co-operating to sponsor the showing.

Timewise, the arrangement for a special showing may either be made for a time in which the theatre is usually closed—such as a Saturday morning, or for a short-schedule evening. In the latter case, participants might attend the eight o'clock showing one evening. At the finish of the film, instead of proceeding into the 9:30 showing, the operator would cancel the last showing and bring up the house lights for the discussion to begin. A virtue of this plan over the Saturday morning plan would be that the operator could continue to sell tickets to the eight o'clock showing to any and all comers. After the showing, the general public might be invited to stay for the discussion, if they so desired.

An adequate discussion period with a large group in a theatre would be difficult, but not impossible. If the discussion leader merely stood in front of the audience, asking questions about the film and letting people respond from any seat in the theatre, not very many persons would have the benefit of becoming directly involved in the discussion. A more widely-involving method would be to use an approximation of the old "Phillips Sixty-Six" method, in which the first three persons on the first row turn to form a buzz group with the first three persons on the second row behind them, and so on across the room. As the moderator poses the questions for discussion, each group goes to work discussing them in their six-man group. After six minutes, the moderator calls for representatives from any group to share their best insights with the total group. In this manner, every person in the largest of groups gets to participate directly in the discussion of the film.

The "hiring of the hall" is really necessary only when the group wishes to see a film which has been released only in a 35-millimeter version (for professional machines only) and not yet in the non-commercial 16-millimeter version. It will also be helpful when the group desires to sponsor a *Kirchentag*-like "Community Festival of Faith," in which an effort is made to involve the entire community of church and non-church people by utilizing the open channel of motion pictures as a basis for drawing persons into faith-and-life discussions.

### THE THEATRE PARTY

Actually, a much simpler method than the foregoing for a small group is simply to have a "theatre party." To do this, all members of the group agree to attend a particular showing of a film which is currently showing at a local theatre, then to meet for their discussion in a nearby home or in a room of the church building. The drawbacks to any method of seeing a film in one place, then going to another place to discuss it, must be weighed against its advantages. There is often a loss of much of the vividness of the film's impression in the scramble and hubbub of changing places. Some persons may choose to be "drop-outs" along the way from theatre to discussion place. Also, unless a discerning member of the group has already seen the film and vouched for its discussion value, the group may view a film about which there is little to be said.

SECURING AND VIEWING A RENTAL PRINT

The method of viewing a film which seems to meet best the needs of small-group discussion is the rental of a 16mm print of the film for viewing and discussion at the church building or in some other space which offers adequate facilities. It is surprising how few program leaders in the church are aware that the film which they saw last week on television or last year in the theatre (and wished then that their church group could see and discuss it) is probably now available in a 16mm rental print.

The use of rental prints of films assures a group that it will be able to view its desired film at a time and place convenient to all its members and that members will not have to travel long distances between viewing and discussing. It also opens the door to a rich selection of films which have been released as recently as twelve months ago to as early as 1895! There are film rental libraries in most larger cities (see Appendix III) whose catalogs contain innumerable good films which lend themselves to a realistic investigation of the problems of contemporary living, interpersonal relationships, etc. Many of these libraries are willing to give previews of selected films to a potential user, if he can come to the viewing room at their offices.

Although the rental cost for one viewing of some feature-length films may run as high as $50 and over, a church group whose stated purpose in using a film is study rather than money-raising, and which charges no admission fee for film showings, may qualify for a "sliding scale" of rental fees which is offered by many film rental agencies. Thus, a group of less than 100 persons could obtain a black-and-white, regular-screen (not Cinemascope version, which requires a special lens, lens adapter, and a wide screen) feature for as little as $20 per showing, with proportionately higher fees for larger groups. A study of the catalogs of several film libraries will turn up many films that can be of great value to a group—ranging from the old classics to the latest releases (see Appendix IV).

There are three important considerations which should be kept in mind regarding the private screening of a 16mm print of a feature film:

A motion picture with the integrity to present life as it really is can help persons to discover for themselves how a 2,000-year-old gospel "comes alive" in situations of life in the world today.

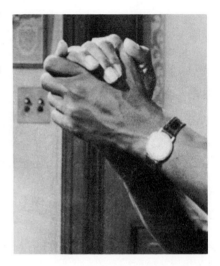

*A Raisin in the Sun* (St. Clement's Film Association)

## 1. Space

The most important factor in choosing space for a film showing is acoustics. The only way to find out about acoustical conditions is to try the space out beforehand, remembering that a people-filled room will have much less reverberation than the same room when empty, and that sound volume will therefore be less with a full room than with an empty room. Because of acoustical considerations, it may be better to use a too-large room if that space has a good public address system or better natural acoustics than a smaller room better suited to the size of your group. Or, if the larger rooms available have poor acoustics, it may be better to have the showing in a much smaller and less glamorous classroom where the sound will have a better chance. Nothing will ruin a film program faster than poor acoustics.

Within the limitations set by the over-arching necessity for good sound, arrangements should be made to have the viewing room as comfortable as possible regarding ventilation, heating or cooling, darkness, seating arrangement, screen visibility from all seats, etc. Viewers should be able to forget completely all of these circumstances as they become involved in the film. These arrangements should be checked out at least twenty-four hours before the viewing, in case some unforeseen problem arises.

It will also be necessary to arrange for separate rooms for each follow-up discussion group. Ideally, these rooms should be as comfortable as possible, with chairs placed in a circle large enough to allow each participant to be on the "front row."

## 2. Equipment

A dependable 16mm sound projector, a large screen in good repair, and a well-qualified projectionist are the basic requirements in this area. The projectionist should have extra projection and exciter lamps on hand in case one burns out during the viewing. The equipment should be set up before the showing begins, including focusing the picture and regulating the sound level. Reels of film should be placed so that the projectionist can find them quickly in the dark for reel changes. If it can be arranged to have two projectors, one projector can be cued up and waiting at all times, thus doing away with the usual problems of turning lights on and off for reel changes, loss of continuity, or people wandering off between reels.

## 3. *Time*

No matter how thorough the preparations, if adequate time is not set aside for a complete program, the whole operation may be a failure. Find out the running time of the film which is to be shown (the film catalog will tell you). Add five or six minutes to this for an introduction, another six or eight minutes for reel changes (unless you plan to use two projectors), ten minutes or so for a "stretch break" between the film and the discussion, and *at least one hour* for the discussion. Adding these, the usual film program will average about three hours, including both viewing and discussion. It should be fully understood by all potential participants at the time that the invitation to view is made that they are contracting to come and stay for the full length of time required for both the viewing *and* the discussion. In fact, a good rule to repeat often is "nobody sees the film who is not willing to stay and discuss it afterward."

If a three-hour stretch of time does not seem feasible for a group, there are some other options. One is viewing the film one evening, then returning to discuss it the next evening. One advantage to this option is that the viewers may be able to "mull over" the issues and images of the film in the intervening time. But the obvious disadvantages are the possible loss of clarity in recollecting the film, and the failure of some persons to return for the all-important discussion. Another option is that of seeing one or two reels of the film (most feature-length films come in three or four 30-minute reels) and then discussing these reels only, returning the next evening to see and discuss the last two reels. This may be the only way a group could find to deal with such long films as *The Diary of Anne Frank*. However, this method may bring about a loss of continuity and ability to appreciate the film as a unit.

Of course, if a group shows signs of being willing to devote extended time to the venture of film study, the ideal arrangement might be to schedule a four- or five-evening "Film Festival" in which the hours from 6:30 to 10:00 are set aside each evening for viewing and discussing films. An even more intensive experience would be to plan a week-long or weekend-long "Film Ministry Workshop" in which participants might devote twelve hours a day to an intensive experience of viewing, discussing, and hearing lectures on the film and the church.

### CONDUCTING A FILM DISCUSSION

Although a film can be adequately viewed by hundreds of persons in a large group, it can be adequately discussed only by a small group of from five to fifteen persons (unless one uses the "66" method described earlier). The reasons are obvious: people have a tendency to "clam up" when they are in a large and therefore "threatening" group. They are less liable to share their deepest feelings and tentative perceptions, as well as their questions, in a large group. Add to this the advantage that the smaller the group, the more time each person will have to express his views.

Just having a small, intimate group present following the showing of a stimulating film does not assure an adequate discussion, however. Groups must have leaders of particular preparation and qualifications. After determining approximately how many people may participate in the film program, enough small-group leaders should be selected so that there will be one leader for every fifteen persons or less. These small-group leaders should be given copies of the film discussion guide (either a general guide such as the one suggested in the next section or the specific guide for that film—see Appendix IV) and, preferably, the opportunity to preview the film together, discussing it afterward just as they will discuss it later with their own groups. Those selected as group leaders should be—or be willing to become—non-directive in their leadership, more anxious to listen than to be heard, and appreciative of every person's contribution no matter how awkwardly put; they should use the humble approach of "a learner among learners," rather than that of a "fountain of wisdom."

Any time spent working with leaders on the group discussion process would be well-spent, particularly if the leaders are new to such a role. The following main points of good discussion leadership might be emphasized: (1) draw out the group members by sensitive use of elicitive, thought-provoking questions rather than by authoritative statements; (2) the leader can help create a climate of acceptance and permissiveness, in which there is no such thing as a "stupid" question or answer; and (3) the big questions of life are much more creative and helpful as end-products of the discussion than are some pat answers. With group members who are not accustomed to the kind of Christian charity which must be practiced by each member if all are to be heard, a group leader might help his group to become aware of this dimension by proposing—at least for the first discussion session—that each person's remarks must bear directly upon the remarks of the previous speaker. Beware of the use of theological jargon, unless it is re-interpreted for the group in a life-centered manner.

In introducing a film to the total group before the showing, the appointed leader should avoid saying anything that will preclude the viewers' own interpretation of the film. There should be no heavy-handed directions as to what to look for. Instead, the leader can simply alert the viewers to the fact that the film is being shown, not as mere entertainment, but as a medium through which God himself may be speaking to his church about her responsibilities in the world. Even if the group has already seen the film before (but only as entertainment), this point of view should make a great difference in what the film may be able to say to the group the second time around.

### AIDS TO "BREAKING OPEN" A FILM

Even if a specific discussion guide prepared for a particular film is not available, groups may still be able to dig into a film by using a system of questioning which will fit any relevant film. These questions, on three successive levels, are designed to lead the group from unthreatening recollection of the content and form of the film, in which everyone gets the feel of participation, toward a genuine searching for relevance and self-examination.

A. Questions to help participants recall and examine objectively the film's form and content:

1. Which scene do you recall most vividly?
2. Were you ever aware of unusual transitions between scenes? Were they appropriate?
3. What use of music do you recall? Did it improve or hinder your experience of the film?
4. Were the actors well suited to their parts? Were you often conscious that these *were* actors acting?
5. Which minor character do you remember strongly?
6. Which setting do you remember vividly? Why?
7. Was the film mainly reliant upon the visual for its impact, or was it mainly verbal?
8. Were you ever disturbed or distracted by various camera angles or movements? Or the lack of them?
9. Was the lighting adequate and appropriate to the moods? (Effective wrestling with questions like these presumes the discussion leader's ability to interpret briefly to group members the criteria for film forms, if they are not already familiar with such norms. By the time these questions have circuited the group a few times, almost the entire picture will have been brought back into the group's consciousness, and everyone will have had the chance to get the feel of participation.)

B. Questions that help the group members to clarify their subjective reactions to characters and situations:
1. Do you recall your own moods while watching?
2. Do you recall any times when the group laughed nervously? Whole-heartedly?
3. To which character were you drawn, at what place in the film? Did your attitude change at any point?
4. Did you become angry with any of the characters? Why?
5. Were you ever uneasy with any of the characters? At what point?
6. Were there any characters or scenes that strongly repelled you? Which ones?

C. Questions that bring to bear the language-symbols traditional to the Christian faith:

*La Strada* (St. Clement's Film Association)

1. Where was "sin" occurring in this film?
2. Where did you see "grace" in this film?
3. Did you see any "divine activity" going on?
4. Where did you see the "Christ-Event" in this film? That is, where did you see someone presented with an opportunity for realizing the "saving truth" about who he really is, an opportunity for finding a new relationship with himself and others?
5. Where did you see "death and resurrection" in the film? That is, where did you see a dying to an old, phoney way of living and an emergence into a new way of living—from brokenness to wholeness?
6. Through whom did Christ seem to minister to others?
7. Would you say that this picture was "religiously significant" or not? Why?

### A SHORT CHECKLIST OF CRITERIA FOR FILM SELECTION

After reading about a film or previewing it, the best way to determine whether or not it would be a good dialogue-feeding film for a group might be to ask several questions:

1. Is it true-to-life? That is, are its characters fully human, rather than stereotyped, and do they find themselves in situations and conflicts which well might happen to such persons under the circumstances?

2. Does the film deal *seriously* with the problems and challenges which it raises? Or does it offer pat answers or too-easy resolution of difficult issues?

3. Does the film clarify for the audience some really important problem or dimension of human relations, self-understanding, etc., or is it content to deal with superficialities?

4. Is the importance of what this film might lead the group into dealing with commensurate with the expenditure of time and money which it will require?

5. Would the use of *this* film at *this* time with *this* group be appropriate to the purpose of creative dialogue?

No one knows how many promising programs of film studies in local churches have been nipped in the bud by an insensitive

selection process. When a congregation has not yet been exposed
to the idea of a film as God's summons to the church to get out
into the world to meet an agonizing need, or as a presentation in
secular form of the gospel as it meets a human situation, then it
may be wise to begin such a program with a meaningful but
non-controversial film, such as *Edge of the City, Bad Day at Black
Rock,* or *The Ox-Bow Incident,* rather than *Cat on a Hot Tin
Roof* or *La Dolce Vita.* It is also good to begin with more straightforward, pedestrian films rather than with the more symbolic and
involved presentations, such as the films of Bergman and Fellini.
The latter are certainly good and most useful, but probably belong
(except with an already highly sophisticated group) in the "ad-
vanced studies" category.

*The Red Balloon* (A Brandon Films 16mm Release)

# 6. USING THE SHORT FILMS

There are many conditions under which the use of a feature-length film will be impractical. If the benefits of the filmic experience are desired for a situation in which a group's time or finances are severely limited, it is still possible to provide this experience through short films of value.

When one begins to consider the use of shorter films, the range of possibilities is bewilderingly expanded to include documentary films, industrial films, promotional films, educational films, experimental films, etc. Almost all of these types of films are produced only in 16mm versions, and are available for rent (industrial and promotional films are usually available on a free-loan basis) at considerably less cost than feature films. They may be obtained through rental agencies, local public library audio-visual departments, or audio-visual departments of state universities. Many regional denominational education offices are beginning to build their own film rental libraries out of short films which have recurring demand among church groups.

Although the short films are difficult to assign to any hard-and-fast categories, those of special significance for the church within the context already set in preceding chapters in this book (and excluding the more obvious uses of the educational film) fall rather arbitrarily into two main classifications: documentary and experimental.

### THE DOCUMENTARY FILM

By the documentary film is meant all methods of recording on celluloid any aspect of reality interpreted either by factual shooting or by sincere and justifiable reconstruction, so as to appeal either

to reason or emotion, for the purpose of stimulating the desire
for, and the widening of, human knowledge and understanding,
and of truthfully posing problems and their solutions in the spheres
of economics, culture and human relations.[6]

This definition of documentary film, drawn up by the World
Union of Documentary in 1948, points up the main distinctions of
this type of film. First, its intent is to present reality, rather than
fancy. In the early '20's when the documentary movement was
building up steam under the guidance of Robert Flaherty (*Nanook of the North, Moana, Man of Aran*), it was given impetus by
its strong reaction against the then highly unrealistic story-films of
Hollywood. Men like Flaherty believed that the actual experiences
of real men were not only just as exciting and view-worthy as any
fanciful screenplays, but that they had the added advantage of
being able to elucidate the life of *all* men through their cinematic
concentration upon the lives of *some* men.

The second foundation principle of documentary lies in its stern
demand for the real experiences of real people in their real environ-
ments. A genuine documentary film will "stage" its action only
when absolutely necessary, and then usually with non-professional
actors in their natural settings, and with every attempt at "sincere
and justifiable reconstruction" of the actual event.

No film, not even newsfilm, can claim to be a completely
objective and non-interpretive representation of a real event.
What the cameraman chooses to shoot and not to shoot, and the
angles and lighting which he uses put the stamp of his own
concerns and prejudices upon the film. The editor then interprets
and editorializes by the manner in which he uses some shots for
the finished film, but leaves others on the cutting-room floor. The
editor also interprets the material by the manner in which he
juxtaposes certain bits of film with other bits of film, and by the
techniques with which he joins them. Finally, the words and
music—even to the nuances of the narrator's voice—subjectively
distort the objective facts. The third principle of documentary,
then, is not a claim to objective reporting, but a zeal on the part of
its makers for as much truthful "posing of problems and their
solutions" as is humanly and cinematically possible. A good exam-

ple of this zeal was Flaherty's practice of living for several months among the people and situations he planned to photograph before he ever shot his first frame. His purpose in doing this was to divest himself of the attitudes, prejudices, and desires which he consciously and unconsciously brought to the subject, in an attempt to let the subject dictate its own genuine nature to him and—through him—to the film. It should be added that not all documentary film-makers have adhered so faithfully to the basic "ethic" of documentary as did Flaherty. The documentary appearance has been crassly misused by many governments and industries (and even denominations) for their own, obviously propagandistic purposes.

In a time like today, when the church is beginning once again to realize its total responsibility for all orders of life in the world outside its walls, documentary films can afford indispensable clues for the church's ministries. They can be not only channels through which the world can speak of its ills and woes to the church, but also they can afford church people vicarious, empathetic experiences of what it looks and feels like to be in the shoes of the outcast, downtrodden, and neglected elements of society.

If an urban congregation, for instance, senses its need to minister more effectively to the life of its city, a good way to begin strategizing for such ministries is to study such perceptive film documents as *The Changing City; How to Look at a City; The Newcomers; Good Night, Socrates;* or *Harlem Crusader.* Coupled with field trips and fact-finding about their own particular city, such films can add vital elements of information and motivation to such a budding ministry. The motivational power of the documentary lies in its ability to make everyday life and accustomed scenes into drama by its creative interpretation of reality.

Another of the varied areas of ministry in which documentary films can help to illuminate and sensitize their viewers is family life. In the case of films like *Angry Boy* and the Dutch production *The Umbrella,* the viewer is not only informed objectively by being shown conflicts between parents and children, children and their siblings, but is also able to gain a vicarious experience of the inside of the troubled child's emotions and attitudes. Thus, not only do the viewers of such films become intellectually informed, but also emotionally sensitized to a problem in the world which begs for ministry.

### THE EXPERIMENTAL FILM

This classification of motion pictures is often used as a "trash basket" category into which are thrown all films which do not lend themselves obviously to the more well-defined pigeonholes of "feature," "educational/instructional," "industrial/promotional," or "documentary." Experimental films originally began, as did the documentary films, as a protest and antithesis to the story-films. But, whereas the direction of the documentary was toward objective reporting of the actual scene, the direction of the experimental film has been toward a very subjective form of self-expression, or a highly imaginative recording of impressions made upon the filmmakers by colors, forms, ideas, relationships, moods, etc. In breadth, these films may range from a montage of black and white shots of city traffic (N.Y., N.Y.: A Day in New York) or children playing in the streets (My Own Yard to Play in) to a fully-animated color film (The Adventures of *) or a series of rhythmic scratchings and daubings of color directly on raw film (Norman McLaren's Begone, Dull Care). In depth, the experimental films may range from those which have the most serious implications for international relationships (Neighbors, A Place in the Sun) to bits of sheer frivolity and joyful abandon (Clowns and Lovers, Orange and Blue). Their importance for the church is unique: their sheer creativity shames us with our dullness; their fragile sensitivity to the subtlest nuances of human aches and hopes reveals our callousness; their deliberate concentration upon the sore spots of today's world forces our attention upon that which we had usually rather ignore.

The best and most serious of the experimental films speak to us in a language that is beyond words, conveying their meanings subtly and implicitly with a poetic imagery that shocks us with recognition of some element of life that we have glimpsed only vaguely before, but never been able to bring to expression. They lift into our shared visual experience emotions, moods, and experiences which we have never dreamed of being able to share, even

Some short films—beneath whose unpretentious surfaces lie depths of implicit commentary upon our human situation.

*Time Out of War*
(Contemporary Films, Incorporated)

*The Hole*
(A Brandon Films 16mm Release)

with those closest to us. The camera or the animator's pen moves in to catch, stop, and scrutinize universal experiences which are usually almost invisible to all but the most perceptive eye and heart. The promise of the unfolding of all the riddles of the universe seems offered to us in every deeply human or universal experience captured by the camera, teasing us into a closer and closer examination. And the closer we look at the most mundane of these little episodes which all our lives hold in common, the closer we may feel we come to the roots of the one, final Reality which lies like a solid bedrock and a fertile soil beneath the experience of every man in every age.

The self-authentication of these little "parables" lies in their susceptibility to such penetrating examination. No matter how deeply and inexorably we probe into the seemingly commonest of them, there is always a further depth to them that remains, beckoning, and always yielding itself to serious and sincere inquiry.

### SOME CONTEXTS FOR THE USE OF SHORT FILMS

Documentary and experimental films can be utilized as elicitive inputs into study programs or even into worship services; but they are also highly useful as total programs in themselves. The following are five contexts for the presentation of such films, with suggestions for their introduction and for follow-up discussions. It should be kept in mind that, in every case, the leader's own words are more helpful to his group than the mere repetition of the following models of introductions, and that questions which apply more specifically to the study area, problems of locale, and type of group are always more useful than the general questions proposed here.

## 1. The World Speaking to the Church

A. BACKGROUND FOR INTRODUCTION: That favorite New Testament verse of Christians, John 3:16, says in no uncertain terms that "God so loved the *world* . . ."; the New Testament delights in reminding us again and again (lest we forget) that we Christians are called by God—every one of us—to serve the *world*. In fact, the Bible is very clear that the whole purpose of God's bringing the church into being was certainly not to serve itself, but to serve the world. What goes on inside the church, then, must necessarily be primarily for the benefit of those on the outside of the church—for those adrift in this world that God so loved, and continues to love.

But how are we to know what the needs of the world are? We are always *assuming* that we know, and then speaking to the world, but on our own terms. The world must learn our language before it can hear our message, we seem to insist. It must ask only the questions for which we have ready-made answers, we imply by such presumptuousness. But, because we are not bothering to listen first to the world before we attempt to speak to it, the world may not listen to us very seriously.

If we would truly serve the world, we need to stop our incessant gabbling for awhile and have the humility at least to listen to our poor patients before we attempt to prescribe for them out of the riches of God's wisdom. We need to say, "World, what are your crying needs? Tell us—in your own terms—and we will try to listen and understand." If we truly do this, perhaps we shall even hear God speaking to us from "out there," calling us to our task.

Let us watch this short film, then, that seems to be a spokesman for a needy, perplexed, but demanding world.

B. POSSIBLE FILMS: *Have I Told You Lately That I Love You?*; *Time Out of War*; *Good Night, Socrates*; *Detached Americans*; *A Place in the Sun*; *Willie Catches On*, etc.

C. POSSIBLE QUESTIONS FOR DISCUSSION:

Which of its needs, hopes, or fears was the world pointing out to us in this film?

Do you think the film presented a true picture of the way things are?

What might God be calling us, the church, to do about this situation? What ought we to say to, and do for, these people?

2. *Standing in Someone Else's Shoes*

A. BACKGROUND FOR INTRODUCTION: As Christians, we are called upon to treat every man as our neighbor, and to love our neighbor as we love ourselves. But how are we to love our neighbor, whose mind, background, and circumstances we do not know, even as we love ourselves about whom we do know all these things (albeit imperfectly)? It is in response to this kind of a need that we can see how a man of faith is called to develop his talents for empathy—for "feeling-with" another person—for developing the kind of an imagination with which he can put himself in the other's shoes. Then, and only then, can the Christian be somewhat more aware of how to go about answering his neighbor's need.

Here is a sensitive film which offers us precisely the opportunity we need; that is, an empathetic, vicarious experience of the *inside* of another's life. It offers us an experience without which we'd hardly be able to imagine his real needs, an experience which we would also not usually find available to us in a more *direct* manner.

B. POSSIBLE FILMS: *The Umbrella*; *My Own Yard to Play in*; *Angry Boy*; *Grassroots*; *Boy with a Knife*; *Children Without*, etc.

C. POSSIBLE QUESTIONS FOR DISCUSSION:

Did this motion picture give you an insight into this person's life you might not otherwise have had?

As a Christian, what do you have to say to this person—to those causing his suffering?

Does this film illuminate some aspect of your own existence? What does it say to you?

Do you feel that you might be better able to minister to such a person after having seen this film?

## 3. *Films That Preach the Gospel—Celebration*

A. BACKGROUND FOR INTRODUCTION: "The earth is the LORD's, and the fulness thereof." [7] For the Christian, "the whole earth is full of [God's] glory" [8]—or should be. And we should also be able to discern that "all his works praise him."

Our trouble, however, is that we are usually so busy over many things that our eyes are blind and our hearts hard to the multitude of *common* gifts of God's grace. We see them, but do not notice them; we use them, but do not rejoice in them. What can make us sensitive to the wonder and sheer blessing of the *everyday* gifts of the Father—like water, or bread, or even glass? Far from such joy in the common gifts of God being optional in the faithing person's life, it is highly necessary. For, in and through these created orders of grace, God is proclaiming to us his message of forgiving, renewing, sustaining love for us. As Paul puts it, "Ever since the creation of the world his invisible nature, namely, his power and deity, has been clearly perceived in the things that have been made." [9]

In the next few minutes, the eye of the motion-picture camera is going to enable us to slow down our customary fast pace, and to concentrate upon the wonder and magnificence of some of the most commonplace of God's gifts—so that we may celebrate them.

B. POSSIBLE FILMS: *Water's Edge, Bread of Paris, Glass, Praise the Sea, Morning on the Lievre, Journey into Spring, A Child's Christmas in Wales, An Occurrence at Owl Creek Bridge*, etc.

C. POSSIBLE QUESTIONS FOR DISCUSSION:

> What was the main impression which the film made upon you?
>
> Did this film enable you to appreciate some common gift of God's grace more keenly? How did it do so?
>
> Why is it that we are so often insensitive to the great gifts that are given to us, like this one?
>
> What would it mean to be able to celebrate the gift of life more continuously—what kind of a person would that make of us?

## 4. *Films That Preach the Gospel—Proclamation*

A. BACKGROUND FOR INTRODUCTION: Jesus said, "I am . . . the truth . . ." [10] And John said of Jesus, "In him was life . . . The true light that enlightens every man." [11] And Christians have the audacity still to claim that Jesus Christ is the Truth—the Truth about life—not only for us, but for every man.

The gospel of Jesus Christ, then, is nothing more nor less than the Truth about life, about every common man's every common moment. And wherever and whenever an artist happens—by accident or by design—to portray the truth about life, he cannot help but "preach the gospel" with the same act.

*The Hole* (A Brandon Films 16mm Release)

Whenever Christ becomes manifest in a work of art, the experience always represents at least one facet of the eternal drama of the meaning of life—the Christ-Event—in a manner similar to the following:

—We see an inauthentic life, in estrangement from God, from others, and from the reality which God gives as a gift of his grace.

—There is a realization of this inauthenticity (unless the realization is rejected) which involves a "death" to the old, estranged life and a turning-toward a new possibility.

—And there is a "resurrection," or a being born again into a new and authentic existence of integrity, love, and responsibility.

We are going to see a short film now, in which some facet of the truth about life—the Christ-Event—is presented in a fanciful but deeply perceptive manner.

B. POSSIBLE FILMS: *The Red Balloon, The Adventues of* *, *A Chairy Tale, Parable, There Was This Carpenter—, White Mane,* etc.

C. POSSIBLE QUESTIONS FOR DISCUSSION:

Did you see anything that might be termed as "sin" in this film? How about "grace"?

Did you see any "death and resurrection"?

Where did you see anything that might be called "divine action"?

Through whom did Christ seem to be ministering?

How did this film illuminate some aspect of social or personal relationships?

## 5. *Films That Preach the Gospel—Prophecy*

A. BACKGROUND FOR INTRODUCTION: An integral part of the preaching of the gospel is prophecy. The prophetic Word is not limited only to the Old Testament, but is also vitally present in the New Testament, as when Jesus prophesies that even the prostitutes and tax collectors will enter the Kingdom of Heaven before the Pharisees will.

Contrary to popular superstition, prophecy is not a mystical or magical seeing into the future much as a crystal ball gazer might do to get a glimpse of tomorrow's racing form. In fact, Paul speaks against this kind of sorcery for Christians in no uncertain terms. True prophecy is, rather, a word pretty much like, "If you don't mend your ways, this is what is bound to happen to you, sooner or later." It is also a means of ripping the customary coverings off our hiding places in order to reveal to us and to the world what we really are.

Certain films have been known to fulfill one or both of these prophetic functions, and thus to preach the gospel—to prophesy. Here is one of them:

B. POSSIBLE FILMS: *Neighbors; A Short Vision; Clay; The Hangman; Come in, Jupiter; The Hole,* etc.

C. POSSIBLE QUESTIONS FOR DISCUSSION:

What was the central "message" of this film?

Was the point of view of the film-maker much different from your own? In what way?

Do you feel more knowledgeable—or alarmed—about this problem than you did before?

Did the film seem to point out any way the problem might be dealt with, its consequences averted? If not, how do you think we might be able to do something about it?

# 7. CRITICAL VIEWING OF TELEVISION

Since its advent as a nationwide medium in the early '50's television has become one of the common denominators of our culture.

> In fact, in the more than 50 million homes equipped to receive television programs, the television set is in use for an average of at least five hours a day, 365 days a year.[12]

Through the "clear channel" which television has blazed into the homes of the nation, hundreds of hours of possible viewing-experiences are set before an entertainment-hungry public each week. Dramas, situation comedies, panel shows, variety shows, soap operas, old and new movies, documentaries, commercials, news, sports, and weather comprise the visual diet of televiewers, giving them an unheralded amount of visual communications. It also gives them a fund of vicarious experiences in common with their fellow-viewers that would have been unimaginable in the days when only the movies afforded such experiences.

Although criticizing television is a popular pastime among church people, there is very little critical viewing—i.e., discerning, discriminating, and evaluative viewing—done by the church. Most people, including church members, communicate with one another about their common televiewing experiences on much the same superficial level as they do about the motion pictures which they see in common. A passive and largely uncritical audience is responsible to a great degree for the quality of both existing and future programming on television. The benefit of most of the existing good programming is lost by a lack of publicizing the programs by their well-wishers, and by a lack of digestive discussion of the programs afterward. Poor programming, on the other hand, is subtly encouraged by careless watching, or by simply tuning it out without any effort at discerning why it is bad or how it could be improved.

Lack of overt support for programs of genuine psychological and humanitarian value, and tacit approval of exclusively escapist diversions, also assures that there will be more and more of the latter type of programs in the future. In every sphere of the public arts, a growth of quality production can be assured only by support and encouragement. Mediocrity is the only thing that flourishes without critical support.

As long as most sponsors and networks continue to make their programming decisions on the basis of audience measurement alone, shows with great potential value to the public, but with small audiences, will continue to fail. Although television is required by the Federal Communications Commission to operate "in the public interest," that requirement is usually interpreted by the networks as "what the majority want to see" rather than "what the populace might most benefit from seeing." Various systems of audience measurement employed upon national television programming (Nielsen, Trendex, etc.) indicate a stronger and stronger trend toward what Hollywood television producers frankly call "escape-pieces" and away from what they call "think-pieces."

There is nothing essentially wrong with escapism. In fact, a little escape every now and then provides a very necessary mental and emotional refreshment. Escapism is a problem only when the escapee does not realize that he is escaping, or when escapism becomes a main diet—almost a way of life. When almost the total program time of the television medium becomes taken up with escapism, there is a problem.

Any group of people, therefore, who believe that television can better serve the people with more interpretations of reality and less escapism have a mandate to do something about prevailing conditions of television programming. Not very many persons in the United States would like to suggest the nationalization of networks as an answer to the problem. (BBC in Great Britain, the government-operated network, provides a wide variety of cultural programs, whether the public watches them or not. But even there, there is now a rise of the independent networks, with their ways of determining program content similar to the methods used in the U.S. It is only in the Iron Curtain countries that the government excludes the right of independent commercial broadcasting.) The only other solution seems to lie in the development of a more discriminating audience. And what national organization could better take upon itself such a project than the church, which has one or more outposts in every hamlet in the country? A medium with as great a potential for information and illumination as television deserves and demands an audience which will continually push it toward its fulfillment as a creatively responsible factor in society. Such an audience will need to be (1) able to deal creatively and appreciatively with the best offerings of the medium; (2) discerning and adept in pointing very specifically to the faults of inferior offerings; and (3) in communication with the decision-makers of the industry.

### DEALING CREATIVELY WITH TELEVISION'S BEST OFFERINGS

Every congregation should have a regular channel of advance information on television programming. The weekly television guide of newspapers comes too late to enable wise planning for group television viewing. Some denominational periodicals now provide a monthly preview of future programming which may be of value to their members. Another source of information is the networks themselves. Both CBS and NBC have regular mailings of advance program information which they send to organizations requesting the service. (Write to CBS Reference Dept., 485 Madison Ave., New York, N.Y. 10022, and NBC Press Dept., 30 Rockefeller Plaza, New York, N.Y. 10020.) The networks co-operate to maintain a Television Information Office (666 Fifth Ave., New York, N.Y. 10019) which sends free mailings of advance program information on all networks to those institutions requesting it. Many local television stations also have a monthly mailing list of advance information for their channel.

Church-oriented advance reviews of selected television programs are provided in the bi-weekly newsletter of Mass Media Ministries (2116 N. Charles St., Baltimore, Md. 21218, $7.50 per year). Advance program information and also guides for group discussion of occasional relevant programs are provided to members of the Saint Clement's Film Association (423 W. 46th St., New York, N.Y. 10036, membership $10 first year, $5 for each year thereafter).

With such advance notification, churches should be able to notify their members of important future programs, suggesting that they view them. Churches should also be able to come up with some thought-provoking, evaluative questions (similar to those proposed in Chapters 5 and 6) to offer to their members as a guide for their discussion of the programs after they view them. Such discussion guides, when published in a church's weekly newsletter, would be of great benefit to family groups watching at home. After the program, they could turn off the set and launch into a genuinely adequate discussion of the program among themselves, with even the children and youth participating.

Of course, it is also possible to have larger discussion groups viewing and discussing selected programs. Publicize in a newsletter that several homes will be open at a designated time, with set and coffee pot on, and with a discussion leader. Because so many families own lightweight portable television sets, it may also be possible to have an entire congregation view a television program in the church's building by breaking up into small groups, each with their own room, receiving set, and leader (with guide).

Programs which lend themselves best to such group viewing and discussion are the occasional "special" dramas which are likely to meet the same criteria suggested for motion pictures at the end of Chapter 5. Segments of continuing shows which have a "confrontive" approach (such as the late, great *East Side, West Side* and *The Defenders*) will also be useful, as will socially-important documentaries (the NBC *White Papers*, for example) and, of course, the best of the old movies. Replays on television offer a congregation the opportunity to see and discuss a motion picture which they feel they cannot afford to rent (but the price may be paid in exasperating commercial interruptions).

### DEVELOPING A DISCERNING AUDIENCE

The benefits of televiewing lie not only in watching and discussing the realistic and seriously probing "think-pieces." An equal, if not greater in some cases, benefit will accrue to a group which watches and discusses critically some "escape-pieces," and even commercials.

After viewing a top-rated program of the "escape" type, a group might deal with questions similar to the following:

Why is this show so popular with such a large percentage of the viewing public?

In its effort to provide laughter (or excitement), did the script remain loyal to basic truths of life? If not, what were some of its distortions?

What image of the father was presented? Of the mother? (Or male-female?) Of youth or children? Are these true?

What did this show seem to suggest as the highest fulfillment of life? Do you agree?

Is the escapism presented here of the beneficial kind, giving a relaxing and refreshing change, but making no attempt to pass itself off as reality—or not?

What does the fact that so many people watch this show faithfully each week say about our society?

A constructively critical approach can also be taken toward television commercials. There is more and more suggested regulation each year regarding truth of claims, number of commercials allowable during breaks, loudness, etc., but there are still as many examples of poor ethical practices in television advertising as there are instances of good ethical practices. Every televiewer should be able to point cogently to the difference between the two kinds, discerning the shades of gray in between. Training in this kind of discrimination might be had by watching commercials together, then discussing such questions as:

What was the motivation used in this commercial? Did it seem to appeal to one motive, yet actually appeal to another, more subtle, motive?

Was this basically an honest statement or appeal? If not, how was it dishonest?

What do you think of the use of this kind of motivation in advertising this kind of product? What might be a more appropriate appeal?

What was the feeling toward the product and the sponsor engendered in you by this commercial?

Do you feel that the commercial had value as an artistic creation (creative use of camera, editing, etc.)?

What usually leads you to call a commercial "a good one" or "a bad one"? Do you think the ones you call "good" are also the ones most effective in selling the product, or not?

If a group has access to one of the home television recorders (Sony now makes one which sells for under $1000), it will be able to record the commercial and play it back several times in succession for a keener impression. If such a video recorder is available, it can also be used to record a pertinent program which comes at an awkward hour and replay it at a more convenient time for a small group.

COMMUNICATION WITH TELEVISION'S DECISION-MAKERS

Ultimately, any effort toward creating a more sensitive and discriminating television audience may eventuate in an effect upon the ratings which, in turn, may bring about programming changes. However, there is a quicker and more direct way to put to use whatever insights may be gained from audience training— letter-writing to the networks and sponsors.

If you are thinking that your one letter won't accomplish anything, remember that few programs receive much mail. At the peak of its popularity, when it reached 47 million persons, *Gunsmoke* averaged only 25 letters a program—about .0000531 percent of its viewing audience. And a few years ago, another program was put off the air for several weeks because of "public indignation"— which turned out to be 300 letters! [13]

Because networks and sponsors usually do not get much mail on their programs, what they *do* get seems to be influential out of all proportion to its percentage of the total viewing audience. Letters

which are not very influential, however, are those which are unspe-
cific, failing to name the program and date of showing correctly, or
rambling about many general issues rather than pinpointing specific issues. *Negative* letters also usually have less effect than letters
which are in support of a particular program, and which are able to
be appreciative of specific issues, acting and writing jobs, direction,
etc. Mass-produced or obviously "form" letters are also singularly
unproductive of change. Letters to networks and sponsors, even
when written by members of a group at a group meeting, should
be written on personal stationery and with one's own personal
style of wording and message.

Letters may be most helpful in supporting certain programs and
in correcting the faults of others if they are directed either toward
the network which airs the show or to the sponsor of the show.
The local station may pass along the word to proper network-level
offices; but it is best to write directly. For specific names and
addresses of sponsors secure a copy of the current *National Television Advertisers* (send 50¢ to American Council for Better Broad-
casts, 423 Pinckney St., Madison, Wis. 53703) or *Sponsors* (send
30¢ to National Association for Better Radio and Television, 573
N. Western Ave., Los Angeles, Calif. 90004).

*The Yearling* (Films, Incorporated)

# 8. CHILDREN, YOUTH, AND THE SCREEN

"But what of the use of motion pictures and television with youth and children?" many readers by now may be asking, with some trepidation. Such a question may well be asked with a bit of fear and trembling in view of the perennial currents of suspicion and hostility about the possible "untoward effects" of the screen media upon children and youth. These currents have run sometimes above ground in loud public outcries, and sometimes underground in a vague, general uneasiness since the birth of these two media. In the early thirties, everyone from sincere parental groups and child psychologists to nut-fringe cranks were waging wars against the movies out of fear of what increasingly frank portrayals of sex and violence might do to children's morals and character growth. When television came on the scene, it received much the same treatment, except added to its condemnation was the fear of what it might do to children's eyes as well as to their morals.

In all of the hue and cry over the possible negative effects of movies and television upon children and youth, the church has more often than not been on the side of potential censors who wanted to protect children and youth from exposure to all possible "corrupting influences."

But what of the implicit claims underlying most censorship movements—that certain books or films have the power in themselves to corrupt those who read or see them? Not half enough research has been done on the accuracy or inaccuracy of suspicions that written or filmed materials can actually influence a child's or a youth's character and actions in anti-social directions; but the great majority of research that has been done in this area makes no strong case for censorship laws. Quite the contrary.

Dr. Paul W. Tappan, sociologist, attorney, and former chairman of the U.S. Board of Parole, stated:

> Evidence is clear that the causes of law violation are to be found deeply rooted in the family and the neighborhood where the child is trained, and not in the movie theatre where he may be entertained.[14]

Dr. Carl Barnhart, child study expert at the University of Toronto, wrote:

> In most cases, by the age of ten, perhaps earlier, whatever character the child has he is likely to have for life—movies, t.v., comic books and the like will be interpreted in the light of these values, attitudes and motives a child has developed in relations with his parents.[15]

Dr. Benjamin Spock, renowned pediatrician, says:

> Most psychiatrists . . . deny that a child who was anywhere normal to start with could be turned into a scoundrel or a thug by any number of hours of viewing or reading. A child acquires his basic standards from his parents.[16]

Dr. Benjamin Bloom, Professor of Education at the University of Chicago, President of the Association for Educational Research, and a member of the standing committee of the International Study of Educational Achievement, also treated the problem of where a child gets his character traits and value standards in his book *Stability and Change in Human Characteristics* (New York: John Wiley Press, 1965). After surveying and synthesizing the findings of all major longitudinal studies, some of which followed particular children for ten or more years, Professor Bloom was able to corroborate the psychoanalytic hypothesis that characteristics acquired early in life are the most stable. He and his co-workers were also able to identify thirteen factors most influential upon the intellectual growth and the establishment of personality characteristics in children. *Every one* of the thirteen factors related either to the family background or to the relationships between parents and children.

In the face of such authoritative statements as the foregoing, it may appear to many that movies and television have long been

scapegoats, receiving the blame for much of the guilt that right-
fully belongs to the home, to parents, and to family-serving agencies (such as the church) which have not been doing their job
adequately. Whenever the church has joined in venting hostility
toward the screen media for causes actually belonging to the
home, it may well have been adding to the smoke-screening of the
genuine issues by belaboring the very tool which it might use to do
something constructive about the real problem.

### MOVIES AS AN ENTRÉE TO CROSS-GENERATIONAL DIALOGUE

Where it has been tried, the use of films which deal frankly and
realistically with parent-child relationships has already been found
to be useful in opening up avenues of communication between
parents and their children. After watching together such films as
*Captains Courageous* or *The Yearling*, parents and their younger
children have been able to find "handles" for talking sympatheti-
cally and in depth to one another about problems of discipline,
rejection, injustice, and hostility. Finding it much easier to begin
talking openly about screen characters than about themselves,
parents and teen-agers viewing *Blue Denim* or *Rebel Without a
Cause* have experienced an unusual degree of communion and
mutual insight while discussing afterward the thorny issues of sex,
freedom, and responsibility, as well as searching together for satisfying images of youth and adult being.

Through careful employment of the common denominator of
shared, vicarious film experiences, the ever-widening generational
gap may be narrowed long enough to allow some fertile moments
for the meeting of minds and hearts.

### MOVIES AS AN AID IN TEEN-AGE SEX EDUCATION

Many persons in our society want to protect youth from fic-
tional treatments of sex, either in books or in films. Their desire
often leads to censorship movements, which attempt to bar youth
from certain books or films. The central tragedy of such censorship
movements is that, while they succeed in keeping youth from
seeing the sensationalistic "flesh flicks" (the nude movies shown in
low-class "art film" houses), they also prohibit youth from seeing

some very straightforward and honest motion pictures which deal with the sexual dilemmas of youth with real insight and integrity. In the well-meaning act of trying to protect youth from lies and distortions about life, censors may also protect them from the truths that they badly need to know. Fearing that freedom to read or to see will lead to corruption, censorship movements tend to forget the need for enlightenment, working on "the puritanical fallacy that ignorance is the key to human virtue." [17] Among the obvious drawbacks to this kind of attitude toward youth and sex is ignorance of the fact that a book or a film which deals with sex in a manner that is true to life can help youth to begin thinking seriously and responsibly about sex. What better time is there for such exposure than in the teen years while a youth still has access to the counsel of parents and teachers? Thus he may be equipped with some sound understandings about such human values when he meets the challenge some day—not just in books or films, but in the flesh. A youth will remain in a state of naïveté and misinformation as long as occasions for thinking through the problem of his sexual nature are withheld from him.

As is the case with any kind of film viewing, most of the potential benefit of a realistic motion picture is to be gained in group discussion of its issues and images after the viewing. Without interpretive discussion, the benefit is lost. The film without the discussion seems to have little, if any, lasting impression. Many church groups have been able to utilize fully the potential value of such films as *Splendor in the Grass, Blue Denim,* or *All the Fine, Young Cannibals* by using them as a major ingredient in sex study seminars for youth. The film not only serves to raise the basic questions of youth sexual relationships dramatically and concretely for discussion, but also helps to create a climate of openness and frankness so necessary if youth and their adult leaders are to talk helpfully about any subject of genuine importance.

### FILMS AND YOUTH'S SEARCH FOR LIFE IMAGES

The years of childhood are characterized, in part, by a search for life images. The child's make-believe is an effort to try out many different personalities and attitudes as he unconsciously searches

A dialogue with children can be started with such films as these, which raise the problems of parent-child relations, war, and prejudice.

*The Boy with the Green Hair*
(Films, Incorporated)

*The Yearling* (Films, Incorporated)

A dialogue with youth can be
opened with films such as these,
which raise questions of sexual
ethics and the search for life
images.

*Blue Denim* (Films, Incorporated)

*Hemingway's Adventures of a Young Man* (Films, Incorporated)

for those best suited to his own being. The teen years see an acceleration of this search, adding the quest for "Who shall I be, and what shall I try to be like as an adult?" to the ongoing search for "Who am I now?"

Wherever oppressive and restrictive conditions within a young person's home or social environment limit his ability to search for, find, and project himself into a wide variety of possible life images, there is a consequent restriction of his possibilities for present and future self-fulfillment. Conversely, wherever the opportunity exists for a child or a youth to try on a wide and varied number of self images, the possibilities for his present and future fulfillment are richly expanded.

Many church-related and social service institutions are finding that theatrical motion pictures can be employed as a means of giving children and youth a wider horizon for their search for creative and satisfying life images. The vicarious experience afforded by a well-made dramatic film gives young viewers the opportunity to enter into the action empathetically, and to try out the many personalities, attitudes, and emotions they see enacted upon the screen. In discussion about the nature and intensity of their vicarious experiences after the viewing, these young persons find doors opened to life images they had never imagined before for themselves, and are enabled to make decisions to follow directions which seem fulfilling to them. As in the case of the cross-generational and sex educational uses of the film, it is not the film experiences per se which yield the benefit for the youth, but the depth-level discussions that follow the film viewings. Here are some of the kinds of questions that may be used to aid children or youth in searching out positive and negative life images offered by a film:

How did you feel about this person? Did you like him or not? Why?

Would you like to be a person like that? What problems might you have if you were a person like that?

What could you do if you were a person like that one?

Did this person seem at all phoney to you? If so, when, and what about?

What do you think was most important to him? Do you agree
with him about that?

What could have helped him to be someone more like you'd
like to be?

Films which offer detailed, three-dimensional character por-
trayal, particularly of rather unconventional characters, are useful
for this kind of approach. For youth, such films as *Edge of the
City, Zorba the Greek, Ten Thousand Clowns,* or *Alfie* might be
the type. For children, *Toby Tyler, The Boy with the Green Hair,
A Boy Ten Feet Tall,* or *Captains Courageous* offer some viable
life images for investigation.

### THE NEED FOR SCREEN EDUCATION

Two elements in our society today push us toward a new kind of
education—screen education—in both church and school. One
element is the ever-present uneasiness about the possible negative
effects upon children and youth of films and television. The other
element is the rising tide of audio-visual communications which
are becoming daily a larger part of the world's educational, infor-
mational, and entertainment enterprises.

The only lasting and trustworthy answer to the threat to children and youth which may be posed by those occasional perverse
and distorted pictures of life that come along through screen
media is the fostering of an ability on the part of the young person
to do his own discerning and discriminating between the authentic
and inauthentic, artistic and inartistic, in screen offerings. Similarly, training in awareness of the means and methods as well as in
critical evaluation of screen content seems to be the best way to
prepare this and future generations to be alert and discriminating
toward the visual imagery which will be a larger and larger part of
the human experience.

The answer to both of these problems could be one and the
same—a crash program of screen education such as has been going
on in Great Britain for several decades. Under the direction of the
British Film Institute, teachers of elementary and secondary
schools are given training in the most appropriate uses of film and
television with students. Their training is not only for the purpose

of helping them to use these media wisely in teaching other subjects, but also is aimed at making them capable of teaching film and television arts as subjects worthy of the most intensive study in themselves. A "catch-up" program in the United States could include both schools and churches, with teachers in both institutions learning how to help children and youth to deal creatively, responsibly, and discerningly with man's newest art, and one of his most promising means of communication.

# NOTES

1. John M. Culkin, S. J., "Film Study in the High School," *Catholic High School Quarterly Bulletin*, Vol. XXIII, No. 3 (October 1965), p. 1.

2. Mr. Stanford Summers, Director of St. Clement's Film Assn. New York City (statement in leaflet publicizing the organization).

3. Matthew 13:10, 13.

4. Murray Schumach, *The Face on the Cutting Room Floor: The Story of Movie and Television Censorship* (New York: William Morrow & Co., 1964), p. 17.

5. Ernest Lindgren, *The Art of the Film* (New York: The Macmillan Co., 1963), p. 163.

6. As quoted by Paul Rotha in *Documentary Film* (London: Faber & Faber Ltd., 1952), pp. 30–31.

7. Psalm 24:1 (K.J.V.).

8. Isaiah 6:3b (K.J.V.).

9. Romans 1:20.

10. John 14:6.

11. John 1:4, 9.

12. R. E. Summers and H. B. Summers, *Broadcasting and the Public* (Belmont, Calif.: Wadsworth Publishing Co., 1966), p. 1.

13. "You've Only Yourself to Blame," by the Editors, *Together*, Vol. IX, No. 9 (September 1965), p. 13.

14. Cited by Mrs. Margaret Twyman in a speech at Dallas, Texas, on February 25, 1965, entitled "The Broader View."

15. *Ibid.*

16. *Ibid.*

17. William Iverson, *The Pious Pornographers* (New York: William Morrow & Co., 1963), p. 119.

# APPENDICES

## APPENDIX I: BOOKS AND BOOKLETS FOR FURTHER STUDY

### THE ART OF THE FILM

Bluem, A. W. *Documentary in American Television*. New York: Hastings House, 1965.

*Eisenstein, Sergei. *Film Form and the Film Sense*. New York: Meridian Books, 1965.

Grierson, John. *Grierson on Documentary*. Edited by Forsyth Hardy. Revised Edition. Berkeley: University of California Press, 1966.

*Jacobs, Lewis (ed.). *Introduction to the Art of the Movies*. New York: The Noonday Press, 1964.

*Kracauer, Siegfried. *Theory of Film*. New York: Galaxy Books, 1965.

Lindgren, Ernest. *The Art of the Film*. New York: The Macmillan Co., 1963.

*Montagu, Ivor. *Film World*. Baltimore: Penguin Books, 1964.

*Stephenson, Ralph, and J. R. Debrix. *The Cinema as Art*. Baltimore: Penguin Books, 1965.

Rotha, Paul. *Documentary Film*. London: Faber & Faber, Ltd., 1952.

### HISTORY OF MOTION PICTURES

Fulton, A. R. *Motion Pictures, the Development of an Art from Silent Films to the Age of Television*. Norman: University of Oklahoma Press, 1960.

Griffith, Richard, and Arthur Mayer. *The Movies*. New York: Bonanza Books, 1957.

*Houston, Penelope. *The Contemporary Cinema*. Baltimore: Penguin Books, 1963.

Jacobs, Lewis. *The Rise of the American Film: A Critical History*. New York: Harcourt, Brace & Co., 1939.

*Knight, Arthur. *The Liveliest Art*. New York: Mentor Books, 1959.

*Manvell, Roger. *New Cinema in Europe*. New York: E. P. Dutton & Co., 1966.

Rotha, Paul, and Richard Griffith. *The Film Till Now*. New York: Funk & Wagnalls, 1949.

### FILM CRITICISM

Alpert, Hollis. *The Dreams and the Dreamers*. New York: The Macmillan Co., 1962.

*Kael, Pauline. *I Lost It at the Movies*. New York: Bantam Books, 1966.

---

* Paperback Edition

MacCann, Richard Dyer. *Hollywood in Transition*. Boston: Houghton Mifflin Co., 1962.

Schumach, Murray. *The Face on the Cutting Room Floor: The Story of Movie and Television Censorship*. New York: William Morrow & Co., 1964.

*Taylor, John Russell. *Cinema Eye, Cinema Ear*. New York: Hill & Wang, 1964.

*Warshow, Robert. *The Immediate Experience*. Garden City: Anchor Books, 1964.

SCREEN EDUCATION

Boutwell, W. D. (ed.). *Using Mass Media in the Schools*. New York: Appleton-Century-Crofts, 1962.

*British Film Institute. *Film Teaching*. London: British Film Institute, 1964.

Culkin, John M., S. J. "Film Study in the High School." *Catholic High School Quarterly Bulletin*, Vol. XXIII, No. 3 (October 1965), pp. 1–35.

* Hodgkinson, A. W. *Screen Education*. New York: UNESCO, 1964.

*Mallery, David. *The School and the Art of the Motion Pictures*. Boston: National Association of Independent Schools, 1964.

*McAnany, Emile, and Robert Williams. *The Filmviewers' Handbook*. New York: The Paulist Press, 1965.

*Postman, Neil. *Television and the Teaching of English*. New York: Appleton-Century-Crofts, 1961.

*Sheridan, Owen, MacRorie, and Marcus. *The Motion Picture and the Teaching of English*. New York: Appleton-Century-Crofts, 1965.

## APPENDIX II: SOURCES OF FILM DISCUSSION GUIDES

*Center for Film Study*, 21 West Superior St., Chicago, Ill. 60610—A division of the Catholic Adult Education Center of Chicago, this group specializes in providing film study guides for parochial high school and adult groups. The approach of the guides includes an analysis of both the content and the form of selected films. A nominal fee is charged for the guides, which are mostly for foreign films.

*Films, Incorporated*, 425 North Michigan Ave., Chicago, Ill. 60611 (with branches in Atlanta, Boston, Dallas, Hollywood, New York City, Portland, and Skokie, Ill.)—This organization offers free discussion guides, prepared by the author of this book, for over seventy U.S. films which they also rent. Originally prepared for church discussion groups, these guides are also used with hospitals, prisons, high school and college groups, as well as with executive training groups, social service agencies, etc.

*Mass Media Ministries*, 2116 North Charles St., Baltimore, Md. 21218—For members ($7.50 per year fee), this organization provides assistance in booking films, a bi-weekly newsletter with current information and reviews of both films and television, as well as drama and tape reviews. The additional service of providing film study guides is planned for the near future. Mostly U.S. films, both feature and short.

*The Saint Clement's Film Association,* 423 West 46th St., New York, N.Y. 10036—An outgrowth of the exploratory ministries of the St. Clement's Church in Manhattan, near the Broadway theatrical district. For members (Association Fee is $10 per year for the first year; $5 per year thereafter), services are assistance in booking relevant films, a monthly bulletin alerting members to both motion pictures and television programs of concern, and film and television study guides. Both foreign and U.S. films.

*Society for Education in Film and Television in the United States* (SEFTUS), Boston University, Boston, Mass. 02115—This is the U.S. outgrowth of the group of teachers who pioneered screen education in Great Britain. Members receive regular newsletters from the parent organization, as well as an additional U.S. newsletter, plus discussion guides on the form and content of relevant films.

*Teaching Film Custodians, Inc.,* 25 West 43rd St., New York, N.Y. 10036—Directed toward the use of motion pictures in classroom teaching, the guides of this organization are prepared for a series of 20- to 40-minute excerpts from regular feature films. The excerpts themselves are also available for rental from this organization.

## APPENDIX III: FILM RENTAL SOURCES
(Send for catalogs at each address.)

*Audio Film Classics,* 2138 East 75th St., Chicago, Ill. 60649 (with branches in San Francisco and Mt. Vernon, N.Y.)—Foreign and U.S. features and shorts.

*Brandon Films, Inc.,* 200 West 57th St., New York, N.Y. 10019 (with distributors: Film Center, Inc., 20 E. Huron St., Chicago, Ill. 60611, and Western Cinema Guild, 381 Bush, San Francisco, California 94104)— Foreign and U.S. features and shorts.

*Cinema 16,* 175 Lexington Ave., New York, N.Y. 10016—Experimental films.

*Contemporary Films, Inc.,* 267 West 25th St., New York, N.Y. 10001— Foreign and U.S. features and shorts.

*Continental 16,* 241 East 34th St., New York, N.Y. 10016—Foreign and U.S. features and shorts.

*Film-Makers' Cooperative,* 414 Park Ave., South, New York, N.Y. 10016— Experimental films.

*Films, Incorporated,* 425 North Michigan Ave., Chicago, Ill. 60611 (with branches in Atlanta, Boston, Dallas, Hollywood, New York City, Portland, and Skokie, Ill.)—Some foreign films and the largest library of U.S. features. Encyclopaedia Britannica Films, at the same addresses, maintains a large library of documentary and experimental films. Ask for the "Point of View" catalogue for the latter films.

*Ideal Pictures,* 1010 Church St., Evanston, Ill. 60201 (with branches in

Atlanta, Baltimore, Berkeley, Boston, Buffalo, Chicago, Cleveland, Denver, Detroit, Honululu, Indianapolis, Kansas City, Hollywood, Louisville [Ky.], Memphis, Miami, Milwaukee, Minneapolis, New York City, Pittsburgh, Portland, Richmond, Tulsa)—U.S. features and shorts.

*Janus Film Library*, 24 West 58th St., New York, N.Y. 10019—Foreign and U.S. features and shorts.

*Museum of Modern Art Film Library*, 11 West 53rd St., New York, N.Y. 10019—Foreign and U.S. features, shorts, documentaries, and experimental films from 1895 to present.

*National Film Board of Canada*, 680 Fifth Ave., New York, N.Y. 10019— Documentary and experimental films.

*Swank Motion Pictures, Inc.*, 621 N. Skinner Blvd., St. Louis, Mo. 63130— British and U.S. features and shorts.

*United World Films*, 221 Park Avenue South, New York, N.Y. 10003 (with branches in Atlanta, Chicago, Los Angeles, Portland, and Dallas)—British and U.S. features.

## APPENDIX IV: A PARTIAL LISTING OF RELEVANT FEATURES AND SHORTS

### 1. THEME: "CONFRONTATION BY THE TRUTH"

*Bad Day at Black Rock* (print and guide from Films, Inc.)
*Billy Budd* (print and guide from St. Clement's)
*Butterfield 8* (print and guide from Films, Inc.)
*Cat on a Hot Tin Roof* (print and guide from Films, Inc.)
*Diary of a Country Priest* (print and guide from St. Clement's)
*Edge of the City* (print and guide from Films, Inc.)
*The Given Word* (print and guide from St. Clement's)
*God Needs Men* (print and guide from St. Clement's)
*High Noon* (print and guide from St. Clement's)
*The Hustler* (print and guide from Films, Inc.)
*The Informer* (print and guide from Films, Inc.)
*No Exit* (print only from Brandon)
*The Rainmaker* (print and guide from Films, Inc.)
*Seven Faces of Dr. Lao* (print and guide from Films, Inc.)
*The Seventh Seal* (guide from Center for Film Study, print from Janus)
*Sons and Lovers* (print and guide from Films, Inc.)
*The Sound and the Fury* (print and guide from Films, Inc.)
*Sweet Bird of Youth* (print and guide from Films, Inc.)
*The Virgin Spring* (print only from Janus)
*The Visit* (print and guide from Films, Inc.)
*Winter Light* (print only from Janus)

#### SHORT FILMS

*A Chairy Tale* (10 min., Contemporary)

A *Place in the Sun* (5½ min., Films, Inc.)
*The Red Balloon* (34 min., Brandon)

### 2. THEME: "INTEGRITY V.S. EXPEDIENCY"

*All about Eve* (print and guide from Films, Inc.)
*The Americanization of Emily* (print and guide from Films, Inc.)
*Becket* (print and guide from Films, Inc.)
*Bridge on the River Kwai* (print only from Swank)
*Captains Courageous* (for children) (print and guide from Films, Inc.)
*Four Horsemen of the Apocalypse* (print and guide from Films, Inc.)
*I Like Money* (print and guide from Films, Inc.)
*The Informer* (print and guide from Films, Inc.)
*The Little Foxes* (print and guide from Films, Inc.)
*Question 7* (print only from Swank)
*Room at the Top* (print and guide from St. Clement's)
*Some Came Running* (print and guide from Films, Inc.)

### 3. THEME: "JUSTICE AND MERCY"

*Billy Budd* (print and guide from St. Clement's)
*The Caine Mutiny* (print only from Swank)
*Compulsion* (print and guide from Films, Inc.)
*The Hill* (print and guide from Films, Inc.)
*Intruder in the Dust* (print and guide from Films, Inc.)
*The Ox-Bow Incident* (print and guide from Films, Inc.)
*The Savage Innocents* (print and guide from Films, Inc.)
*The Visit* (print and guide from Films, Inc.)

### 4. THEME: "THE MEANING OF DEATH"

*All the Way Home* (print and guide from Films, Inc.)
*Dark Victory* (print and guide from Films, Inc.)
*Ikiru* (guide from Center for Film Study, print from Brandon)
*Macario* (guide from Center for Film Study, print from Audio)
*Wild Strawberries* (print only from Janus)

#### SHORT FILMS

A *Short Vision* (7 min., Films, Inc.)

### 5. THEME: "THE MEANING OF EXISTENCE"

*Alfie* (print and guide from Films, Inc.)
*The Bicycle Thief* (print and guide from St. Clement's)
*A Boy Ten Feet Tall* (for children) (print and guide from Films, Inc.)
*Breakfast at Tiffany's* (print and guide from Films, Inc.)
*Breathless* (print and guide from St. Clement's)
*The Brothers Karamazov* (print and guide from Films, Inc.)

*The Cardinal* (print only from Swank)
*Citizen Kane* (print and guide from Films, Inc.)
*David and Lisa* (print and guide from St. Clement's)
*Death of a Salesman* (print and guide from St. Clement's)
*Flight of the Phoenix* (print and guide from Films, Inc.)
*Hemingway's Adventures of a Young Man* (print and guide from Films, Inc.)
*Hot Spell* (print and guide from Films, Inc.)
*Hud* (print and guide from Films, Inc.)
*The Hustler* (print and guide from Films, Inc.)
*Ikiru* (guide from Center for Film Study, print from Brandon)
*La Dolce Vita* (print only from Audio)
*La Strada* (print and guide from St. Clement's)
*The Loneliness of the Long Distance Runner* (print and guide from St. Clement's)
*The Long, Hot Summer* (print and guide from Films, Inc.)
*Lust for Life* (print and guide from Films, Inc.)
*Night of the Iguana* (print and guide from Films, Inc.)
*Nights of Cabiria* (print and guide from St. Clement's)
*On the Waterfront* (print only from Audio)
*A Place in the Sun* (print and guide from Films, Inc.)
*The Prisoner* (print only from Swank)
*The Razor's Edge* (print and guide from Films, Inc.)
*Requiem for a Heavyweight* (print and guide from St. Clement's)
*Rhapsody* (print and guide from Films, Inc.)
*Summer and Smoke* (print and guide from Films, Inc.)
*Sundays and Cybele* (print and guide from St. Clement's)
*Sweet Bird of Youth* (print and guide from Films, Inc.)
*Toby Tyler* (for children) (print and guide from Films, Inc.)
*Treasure of Sierra Madre* (print and guide from Films, Inc.)
*The Trial* (print only from Brandon)
*Viridiana* (print only from Audio)
*The Yearling* (for children) (print and guide from Films, Inc.)
*Zorba the Greek* (print and guide from Films, Inc.)

SHORT FILMS

*Two Men and a Wardrobe* (15 min., Contemporary)
*White Mane* (45 min., Contemporary)

6. THEME: "RACIAL PREJUDICE"

*Crossfire* (print only from Films, Inc.)
*Gentleman's Agreement* (print and guide from Films, Inc.)
*Intruder in the Dust* (print and guide from Films, Inc.)
*No Way Out* (print and guide from Films, Inc.)
*A Patch of Blue* (print and guide from Films, Inc.)
*The Quiet One* (print and guide from St. Clement's)

A *Raisin in the Sun* (print and guide from St. Clement's)
*Something of Value* (print and guide from Films, Inc.)
*To Kill a Mockingbird* (print only from Swank)
*The World, the Flesh, and the Devil* (print and guide from Films, Inc.)

SHORT FILMS

*Boundary Lines* (10 min., Contemporary)
*Brotherhood of Man* (10 min., Contemporary)
*The Toymaker* (15 min., Contemporary)

7. THEME: "SEX AND FAMILY RELATIONSHIPS"

*All the Fine, Young Cannibals* (print and guide from Films, Inc.)
*All the Way Home* (print and guide from Films, Inc.)
*The Best of Everything* (print and guide from Films, Inc.)
*Blue Denim* (print and guide from Films, Inc.)
*Breakfast at Tiffany's* (print and guide from Films, Inc.)
*Butterfield 8* (print and guide from Films, Inc.)
*The Diary of Anne Frank* (print and guide from Films, Inc.)
*Forbidden Games* (guide from Center for Film Study, print from Audio)
*The 400 Blows* (print only from Audio)
*Hot Spell* (print and guide from Films, Inc.)
*The L-Shaped Room* (print and guide from St. Clement's)
*Period of Adjustment* (print and guide from Films, Inc.)
*The Proud and the Profane* (print and guide from Films, Inc.)
*The Sandpiper* (print and guide from Films, Inc.)
*The Silence* (print only from Janus)
*The Slender Thread* (print and guide from Films, Inc.)
*The Subterraneans* (print and guide from Films, Inc.)
*Suddenly Last Summer* (print only from Audio)
A *Taste of Honey* (print and guide from St. Clement's)
*Tea and Sympathy* (print and guide from Films, Inc.)
*The Woman in the Painting* (guide from Center for Film Study, print from Brandon)
*The Yearling* (for children) (print and guide from Films, Inc.)
*The Young Lovers* (print and guide from Films, Inc.)
*Zero de Conduite* (print only from Brandon)

SHORT FILMS

*The Adventures of * * (10 min., Audio)
*The Most—the Playboy Philosophy* (27 min., Janus)
*The Umbrella* (35 min., Contemporary)
A *Unicorn in the Garden* (9 min., Swank)

8. THEME: "SOCIAL PROBLEMS"

*Advise and Consent* (print only from Swank)
*Animal Farm* (guide from Center for Film Study, print from Contemporary)

*Blackboard Jungle* (print and guide from Films, Inc.)
*The Earth Will Tremble* (print only from Audio)
*The Fountainhead* (print and guide from Films, Inc.)
*The Grapes of Wrath* (print and guide from Films, Inc.)
*A Hatful of Rain* (print and guide from Films, Inc.)
*I'll Cry Tomorrow* (print and guide from Films, Inc.)
*Los Olvidados* (guide from Center for Film Study, print from Brandon)
*No Down Payment* (print and guide from Films, Inc.)
*Nobody Waved Goodbye* (print and guide from St. Clement's)
*The Quiet One* (print and guide from St. Clement's)
*The Rat Race* (print and guide from Films, Inc.)
*Slander* (print and guide from Films, Inc.)
*Sylvia* (print and guide from Films, Inc.)
*The Three Faces of Eve* (print and guide from Films, Inc.)

### SHORT FILMS

*The Big Fair* (10 min., Films, Inc.)
*Happy Anniversary* (12 min., Swank)
*Harlem Crusader* (28 min., print and guide from Films, Inc.)
*My Own Yard to Play in* (16 min., Contemporary)
*The Pond and the City* (16 min., Films, Inc.)

### 9. THEME: "VOCATION AND BUSINESS ETHICS"

*The Best of Everything* (print and guide from Films, Inc.)
*Blackboard Jungle* (print and guide from Films, Inc.)
*Citizen Kane* (print and guide from Films, Inc.)
*Executive Suite* (print and guide from Films, Inc.)
*The Fountainhead* (print and guide from Films, Inc.)
*Francis of Assisi* (print and guide from Films, Inc.)
*The Last Angry Man* (print only from Swank)
*Madison Avenue* (print and guide from Films, Inc.)
*The Man in the Gray Flannel Suit* (print and guide from Films, Inc.)
*Patterns* (print only from Audio)
*The Power and the Prize* (print and guide from Films, Inc.)

### 10. THEME: "WAR AND PEACE"

*The Ballad of a Soldier* (guide from Center for Film Study, print from Brandon)
*The Boy with the Green Hair* (for children) (print and guide from Films, Inc.)
*Children of the Damned* (print and guide from Films, Inc.)
*The Condemned of Altona* (print and guide from Films, Inc.)
*Dr. Strangelove* (print and guide from St. Clement's)
*The Last Bridge* (guide from Center for Film Study, print from Brandon)

*Shane* (print and guide from Films, Inc.)
*The Victors* (print only from Swank)
*The Young Lions* (print and guide from Films, Inc.)

SHORT FILMS AND DOCUMENTARIES

*The Hole* (15 min., print and guide from St. Clement's)
*Neighbors* (9 min., Cinema 16)
*A Short Vision* (7 min., Films, Inc.)
*That War in Korea* (82 min., Films, Inc.)
*Time Out of War* (22 min., Contemporary)

## 11. THEME: "THE ART OF THE FILM"

(Note: Many, if not most, of the films previously categorized are outstanding for their artistic quality, but have been listed according to their content. These films are included primarily for the quality of their form.)

*Abraham Lincoln* (guide from Center for Film Study, print from Ideal)
*Alexander Nevsky* (print only from Brandon)
*An American in Paris* (guide from SEFTUS, print from Films, Inc.)
*Arsenal* (guide from Center for Film Study, print from Brandon)
*Blood of a Poet* (print only from Brandon)
*The Cabinet of Dr. Calgari* (print only from Audio)
*Call Northside 777* (guide from SEFTUS, print from Films, Inc.)
*Cleo from 5 to 7* (print only from Audio)
*A Day at the Races* (guide from SEFTUS, print from Films, Inc.)
*The Desert Rats* (guide from SEFTUS, print from Films, Inc.)
*Down Memory Lane* (guide from Center for Film Study, print from Museum of Modern Art)
*Film and Reality* (guide from Center for Film Study, print from Contemporary)
*Golden Age of Comedy* (guide from Center for Film Study, print from Audio)
*Greed* (guide from Center for Film Study, print from Brandon)
*The Gunfighter* (guide from SEFTUS, print from Films, Inc.)
*Hallelujah* (guide from Center for Film Study, print from Films, Inc.)
*Intolerance* (print only from Audio)
*The Iron Horse* (guide from Center for Film Study, print from Brandon)
*Jules and Jim* (print only from Janus)
*Last Year at Marienbad* (print only from Audio)
*L'Avventura* (print only from Janus)
*La Règle du Jeu* (guide from Center for Film Study, print from Janus)
*Lili* (guide from SEFTUS, print from Films, Inc.)
*Little Boy Lost* (guide from SEFTUS, print from Films, Inc.)
*The Living Desert* (guide from SEFTUS, print from Films, Inc.)

*The Lodger* (guide from Chicago Center for Film Study, print from Museum of Modern Art)

*M* (print only from Audio)

*Mon Oncle* (guide from Center for Film Study, print from Contemporary)

*Mother* (guide from Center for Film Study, print from Brandon)

*À Nous, la Liberté* (guide from Center for Film Study, print from Contemporary)

*October* (print only from Brandon)

*Odd Man Out* (guide from Center for Film Study, print from United World)

*Potemkin* (guide from Center for Film Study, print from Brandon)

*Rashomon* (print only from Audio)

*Red Badge of Courage* (guide from SEFTUS, print from Films, Inc.)

*Scaramouche* (guide from SEFTUS, print from Films, Inc.)

*Seven Brides for Seven Brothers* (guide from SEFTUS, print from Films, Inc.)

*Sunrise* (guide from Center for Film Study, print from Brandon)

*A Tale of Two Cities* (guide from SEFTUS, print from Films, Inc.)

*Throne of Blood* (guide from Center for Film Study, print from Brandon)

*Tillie's Punctured Romance* (print only from Films, Inc.)

*The Tin Star* (guide from SEFTUS, print from Films, Inc.)

*A Touch of Evil* (guide from Center for Film Study, print from Brandon)

*Treasure Island* (guide from SEFTUS, print from Films, Inc.)

*Viva Zapata!* (guide from SEFTUS, print from Films, Inc.)

*When Comedy Was King* (guide from SEFTUS, print from Films, Inc.)

*World of Apu* (print only from Brandon)

SHORT FILMS

*Begone, Dull Care* (9 min., Contemporary)

*Bread of Paris* (16 min., Films, Inc.)

*Case of the Mukkineese Battle Horn* (25 min., Guide from Center for Film Study, print from Audio)

*A Child's Christmas in Wales* (26 min., Contemporary)

*The City* (31 min., Contemporary)

*Conquest of the Pole* (10 min., Audio)

*The Critic* (4½ min., Swank)

*The Day Manolete Was Killed* (21 min., Films, Inc.)

*The Flute and the Arrow* (78 min., Contemporary)

*Glass* (11 min., Films, Inc.)

*The Golden Fish* (27 min., Swank)

*The Great Adventure* (75 min., Contemporary)

*Judith of Bethulia* (40 min., Audio)

*Magic of Melies* (10 min., Audio)

*Nanook of the North* (55 min., Contemporary)

*Night Mail* (24 min., Audio)

*Orange and Blue* (15 min., Contemporary)
*Praise the Sea* (22 min., Films, Inc.)
*The River* (30 min., Brandon)
*Song of Ceylon* (40 min., Contemporary)
*The Telltale Heart* (9 min., Films, Inc.)
*A Trip to the Moon* (10 min., Audio)
*Water's Edge* (12 min., Films, Inc.)
*The Wind and the River* (10 min., Janus)